THE STORY OF
ST. ALBANS

ELSIE TOMS

M.A., PH.D., J.P.,
ALDERMAN OF ST. ALBANS
MAYOR OF ST. ALBANS, 1960–1961

WHITE CRESCENT PRESS LTD
LUTON

FIRST PUBLISHED 1962
REPRINTED 1965
REVISED EDITION 1975
REPRINTED 1985

© 1962 ELSIE TOMS

ISBN 0 900804 28 9

Printed in Great Britain
by White Crescent Press Ltd
Crescent Road, Luton

To

The City of St. Albans

which holds my heart

this book

is dedicated

in token of my devotion.

CONTENTS

ILLUSTRATIONS
after page 56

In the Text

from drawings by the Author

Maps and Diagrams

ACKNOWLEDGEMENTS

My grateful thanks are due to many people, among whom I must specially mention the following:

Mr. Cyril Swinson, without whose generous advice and help this book would never have been published ; The St. Albans City Council, whose archives have been a principal source of information and who have kindly permitted me to use the Arms of the City and several photographs of which they own the copyright ; the Officers of St. Albans Corporation : Miss B. V. Entwistle, LL.B., the Town Clerk ; A. S. Moody, A.M.I.C.E., the City Engineer and Surveyor ; Miss Muriel Wilson, F.L.A., the Chief Librarian of the City ; and Miss Ilid Anthony, M.A., PH.D., Director of Museums, St. Albans ; the late Col. W. le Hardy, County Archivist of Hertfordshire until 1961 ; Col. John Busby, for generously allowing me to quote from his paper on James West, M.P. ; Miss S. M. Glossop, for permitting me to use the etching of the Abbey before restoration, drawn by her great great-uncle, Captain James Gape ; Mr. E. W. Tattersall for his photographs, several of which were specially taken for this book ; Mr. and Mrs. David Gadsby for their help in making the diagram on page 37 and the sketch map on page 198 ; The Times Publishing Company for their permission to use the map on page 3 ; The Earl of Verulam for his permission to use the reproduction of a water-colour painting of sixteenth-century Gorhambury from the Gorhambury Collection ; and finally the numerous St. Albans citizens who have, on many occasions, given me pieces of valuable information from their own memories or those of their forbears, which have helped to build up the picture of the story of the City.

E. T.

CHAPTER ONE

BRITONS AND ROMANS

S T. ALBANS and the district around has been a human habitation since Neolithic times (about 10,000 B.C. to 1,700 B.C.). Worked flints of that age have been found in the neighbourhood, as have relics of later prehistoric times. There is another proof of these ancient peoples in our district, according to Dr. E. A. Rudge*, in the curious pudding-stones of Hertfordshire conglomerate, nine of which are to be seen, according to him, in our area, two in gardens in New Kent Road and Lattimore Road, and one very large one by the bridge over the ford at St. Michael's. He considers these to be direction signs of the Stone Age men, and starting in 1949 has traced them in many places in Eastern England, leading across the countryside towards the sites of some of the oldest settlements known in Britain. They are, in fact, if he is right, our earliest signposts.

But evidence of the presence of Stone and Bronze Age men in the neighbourhood is rare, and it is not until the Iron Age arrived that the trackways across the county were much used. Our local history really begins with the coming of the Belgic tribes from the Low Countries in the early part of the first century before Christ. They entered Hertfordshire from the south-east and settled there. The first important settlement was at Wheathampstead, where they constructed great fortifications, the last portion of which still remains in the Devil's Dyke, bordering the road leading from Nomansland to New Marford. This was the British capital which Julius Caesar stormed in 54 B.C.

The particular tribe which inhabited this district was the Catuvellauni, and they were very far from the "Ancient Britons" of the old history books, which drew a picture of blue-painted savages dressed in skins, far removed from traces

*Statistical Evidence for a Conglomerate Alignment in Essex.

of civilisation. This picture was a long way from the truth. The Catuvellauni were farmers with ample fields and dairy herds. They lived in huts made of wattle and daub. There was considerable contact with the Continent, especially towards the beginning of the Christian era, and they exported leather and corn, importing wine, oil and pottery in return.

After the defeat of the Belgic leader, Cassivellaunus, the tribal capital moved, probably between 15 and 10 B.C., from Wheathampstead to the site of Verulamium, where, at a spot guarding a ford, they founded a town which was so important that Sir Mortimer Wheeler has called it a "prehistoric metropolis". The name must have been something like the word Verulam, since the coins which were minted there bear the word "Ver" or "Verl" ; these coins were of silver and gold, as well as bronze, and were the first British coins to bear the name of a town and its chief. At the end of the first century B.C. the chief was Tasciovanus, and some of the coins from his mint bear the letters "Tasc".

Finds from this British city were turned up by the plough occasionally, before any serious excavation was carried on, but in 1929 the St. Albans City Council acquired from the Earl of Verulam about half the site of the Roman city which took the place of the Belgic capital, and the excavations carried on thereafter showed that the latter had been situated to the west of the later settlement and that it had been a flourishing town with industrial and commercial elements, which enjoyed a considerable degree of civilisation, with a good deal of contact with Continental influences. The fact that it appears to have had much lighter fortifications than Wheathampstead points to a state of peaceful prosperity. The coins bear out this assumption. There appear to have been two mints, one near the River Ver, the other farther west, since finds of fragments of coin moulds were turned up in great quantity when the road from Hemel Hempstead, which ran near the British, and through the Roman cities, was widened in 1956–58. These coins were cast in moulds and then struck with a die bearing the letters or devices. These designs were influenced by Roman and Greek coins, particularly the Philippus, whose pair of horses appears sometimes as one

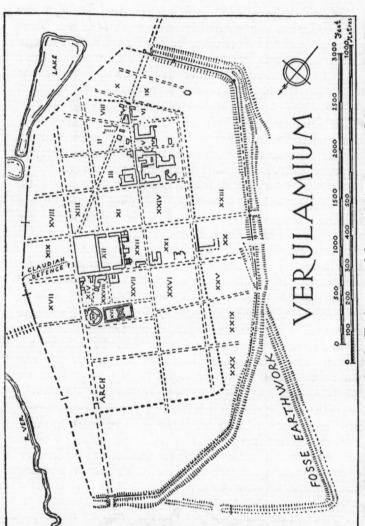

Plan of Verulamium, showing the Flavian town defences within the area of the masonry wall and gateways constructed in the early third century. The "Fosse" earthwork, dated to the early second century, is also indicated.

Reproduced by courtesy of the Verulamium Excavation Committee

horse with six legs.   And it may be noted that the letters
on the coins were Roman in type.

The son of Tasciovanus, Cunobelin (Shakespeare's Cymbe-
line), appears to have ruled over a wide area, as far to the
east as Colchester, where another town was established (later
to be taken over and developed by the Romans as a *colonia*,
or colony of veteran retired legionaries), and this became
the seat of government.   But there is no reason to think that
Verulamium did not retain its importance.   It was still
flourishing when the Romans arrived to conquer, in A.D. 43.

When Cunobelin died his son, Caratacus, renounced his
father's friendship with Rome.   In A.D. 43 Aulus Plautius
was sent to conquer Britain and add it to the Roman Empire.
He captured Colchester and Caratacus fled to the west.
Years later he was captured and sent to Rome, where his
bold bearing roused the respect of the Romans, and he was
released and allowed to return to Britain.   Meanwhile, the
Roman armies had subdued most of the country south of a
line from the Humber to the Mersey.

The Roman authorities appear to have accepted Verulamium as the tribal headquarters, and a new Romanised
city arose not far from the Belgic one, which soon became
deserted as the tribesmen, already accustomed by trading to
certain Continental luxuries, accepted the fleshpots of Rome
and settled down contentedly in the new city.   The historians
used to say that Verulamium was so important that it was
created a *municipium* before the death of Nero.   Of that we
regretfully admit nowadays there is no certain proof, although
it was hoped during the excavations of 1956 that proof would
be forthcoming, when fragments of the inscription set up when
the Forum was completed in A.D. 79 were found.   Unfortunately, the portion which might have confirmed or disproved
the story is missing, so historians can still go on guessing
whether the city was merely a tribal capital or a *municipium*,
whose citizenship carried with it the privileges of which St.
Paul was so proud as a citizen of Tarsus.   One of those who
considers the claim is justified is Prof. Sheppard Frere, who
directed so much of the excavation of the city ; he believes
it to have been one of the Claudian *municipia*.

But tragedy was at hand for the first Roman Verulamium.

In East Anglia, Roman officials indulged in oppression and extortion. Prasutagus, King of the Iceni, had made the Emperor his heir, with his two daughters, since he had no son. He believed that this, in the words of Tacitus, "would put his kingdom and his home out of the reach of wrong". But he was mistaken. When he died the local Roman officials treated his kingdom and his possessions as if they were the spoils of war. When she protested, his wife, Boudicca, was scourged and his daughters violated. Their relatives and chief men were made slaves. Roused to fury and desperation, the Iceni rose in revolt, and led by Boudicca swept down on Colchester, massacred the garrison, and burnt the city. They did the same to London, then, according to Tacitus, undistinguished by the name of *colonia*, but much frequented by a number of merchants and trading vessels. Finally, they passed on to Verulamium and overwhelmed that city also in the year A.D. 61.

The Roman general Suetonius Paulinus came to the rescue. At a place now unknown he faced the Britons. To quote Tacitus again, "Boudicca, with her daughters, in a chariot, went up from tribe to tribe, protesting that it was indeed usual for Britons to fight under the leadership of a woman. 'But,' she said, 'Now it is not as a woman descended from noble ancestry, but as one of the people that I am avenging my lost freedom, my scourged body, the outraged chastity of my daughters. If you weigh well the strength of the armies and the causes of the war, you will see that in this battle you must conquer or die. This is a woman's resolve ; as for men, they may live and be slaves'." Fifteen hundred years later, when Elizabeth I, guarded by some of the men from this very district where Boudicca fought was rallying her countrymen against danger, she might have heard a ghostly whisper in her ears from her great predecessor whose spirit matched with hers. The Romans won an overwhelming victory, and not again did any revolt trouble the Romanised inhabitants of Verulamium, but excavations show lines of burnt building material down in the foundations of the houses and shops built on top of the debris left by Boudicca's hordes.

It has always been considered that there were no forts in early Verulamium, and even the wall was not constructed until the third century. The only defences known were ditches, and the eastern boundary was merely protected by the rich mud of the marshes bordering the River Ver. But excavations carried on in 1961 seem to show that there may have been a fort on that boundary, near the Colchester Gate (near the present St. Michael's Street), though it probably lasted only a very few years, perhaps five, and may have been for policing the transition from Belgic Verulam to the first Roman city, and would have vanished when the area was peaceful and the garrison moved on to less tranquil districts, not to return. On the other hand, it may not have been a fort at all, but a construction camp for the men working on the making of Watling Street. So there is still no evidence of Roman soldiers being stationed at Verulamium, and if there were they were gone almost certainly by about A.D. 50. Had they been there eleven years later Boudicca would not have been able to destroy the city so easily.

Amazingly quickly a new Verulamium rose on the ashes of the first one. It was not exactly on the same site, but extended farther to the south-east, and its area was considerably bigger. Building on a large scale must have begun immediately, and streets of pleasant houses and gardens were laid out, with shops, temples, and at least three triumphal arches and various public buildings, including the civic centre—the Forum—referred to previously. It is evidence of the great prosperity of the city that such a project, probably the culmination of the official development, could be carried out only eighteen years from the destruction of the former city, for the dedication inscription bears the name of Agricola, the general who pacified the country after Boudicca's revolt, and so can be dated precisely. Until the discovery of the fragments of the inscription, it was thought that the Forum was nearly a hundred years later in building. Later on, the citizens had an open-air theatre, not indeed the only one in the province, but the only one which is open to view today. The country-side must have been well populated, to judge by the seating accommodation which was considered necessary. Modern St. Albans has no hall of anything like that size, for all its fifty thousand inhabitants. There were undoubtedly public baths, though their site has not yet been found. They would have been rather like Turkish baths, with rooms of varying temperatures and plunge baths. One, at least, of the private houses had its own bath, and the mosaic floor of one of its series of rooms, with the furnace room and hypocaust, is preserved open to view.

Sometime after A.D. 209 the city was surrounded by a defensive wall, impressive portions of which remain, in the care of the Ministry of Public Buildings and Works. There were four main gates. The south-eastern gate, leading to Watling Street out of the city towards London, has been fully excavated and must have been a very dignified structure, with two carriageways and two passages for pedestrians, flanked by imposing gate-towers and further protected by a fosse or ditch, remains of which are visible today.

Much of the building must have been done with the aid of grants from the Roman authorities. Tacitus tells us that Agricola, who was his father-in-law, gave encouragement and aid, both public and private, to the building of temples, courts of justice and dwelling-houses. He also provided education for the sons of chiefs, and the Britons became anxious to wear the toga. But Tacitus says they also acquired a taste for the things of luxury, the lounge, the bath, the elegant banquet. How much all this Roman luxury corrupted the local lads is problematical.

It is not always appreciated that the Roman rule in Britain lasted for as long as from the reign of the first Elizabeth to the present day, and the traditions of Roman local government went on for even longer, for how long we do not know. During this stretch of time, Verulamium saw changes. For example, in A.D. 155, a part of the city was destroyed by a great fire, which damaged the Forum and swept away buildings, which at this time were mainly timber structures. After the restoration, buildings tended to be of more solid materials, and excavations show strong foundations and walls of flint and strong mortar. Obviously the population was growing in prosperity, and as time went on, more imposing town houses arose with mosaic floors, flint walls and tiled roofs. The theatre was altered in the early fourth century to provide more seating, and even in the late fourth century and early fifth, building was going on, and several large structures were put up.

Inevitably the city declined in prosperity in the end, and the theatre, for some reason, became the refuse disposal dump. Possibly the inroads of the Saxons, when they began to reach the area, made the countryside outside the wall less safe, and the population declined in numbers, which would have the effect of depriving the theatre of a large portion of its clientele. But life and a certain amount of ordered municipal government went on for a very long time, and even in the fifth century, there was sufficient urban life to support a Christian community, educated and sophisticated enough to enjoy a debate on theological schisms when St. Germanus visited the city in 429. Among the audience on that occasion were well-to-do gentry and one man said to be of tribunician rank. Civilisation continued, and even after A.D. 450 clean water was being piped to inhabited buildings, according to Sheppard Frere in his report on the excavations of 1959.

The official withdrawal of the legions to defend Rome itself from the barbarians left the Romanised Britons to carry on the government of the country. There were no forces in Verulamium, and the chief difficulties met with there must at first, at any rate, have been administrative. But eventually they began to experience the inroads of Angles and Saxons, and life inevitably became less safe and peaceful, and it speaks well for the British officials who governed Verulamium that they carried on so successfully for so long.

But how long life went on in the disintegrating city is a matter of conjecture. Coin hoards have been found which appear to have been hidden in the fifth century. I myself do not believe that the site was ever completely deserted until the Saxon abbots demolished the ruined buildings in the tenth century. By the eighth century it must have looked rather like a bomb-site after the 1939-45 War, with some houses down to the ground, others in ruins with bits of wall still standing, and a few still habitable. By that time these were inhabited only by bad characters, footpads and thugs, but that is another story.

The site of Verulamium was never lost, even though in the seventeenth century a writer spoke of it as a "forgotten citie sometimes neare St. Albones". Chauncy, the great late seventeenth-century writer on the historical antiquities of

Hertfordshire, speaks of "the great City of Verolam, where
Cassibelan kept his Court and was afterwards made a Free-
city of the Romans, but since destroyed, so that nothing remains
thereof, more than the Foundation of the Walls, with the
Marks of the Ditches that enclosed about four hundred and
fifty Acres of Ground ; which shewed the Extent of the City
and also the Borough of St. Albans, which was built out of the
Ruins of it, and is scituated within this Liberty".

During Saxon times the remains were subject to destruction
by Saxon abbots, the Normans used it as a quarry for materials
to rebuild the Abbey, and thereafter it was plundered when
anybody wanted bricks. Stukeley, in the early eighteenth
century, said that hundreds of bricks had been taken to mend
roads, and many old garden walls to this day show fragments
of Roman tiles. There is one in Gombards Alley where they
show clearly. These were probably made at the brick kiln
discovered some years ago at Park Street, on the outskirts of
St. Albans. In the excavations many pieces of wall were
found with the brick courses completely gone, leaving a flat
top of cemented rubble.

CHAPTER TWO

ST. ALBAN. THE SAXON MONASTERY

As in all parts of the Roman Empire there were many
religious sects to be found in Britain. There were
several temples in Verulamium, though we do not
know to what gods they were dedicated. One assumes that
there must have been some followers of Mithras from the fact
that a Mithraic symbol has been found. There were also
some Christians, and one of them became the first British
Christian martyr, St. Alban. He was to give his name to the
Saxon village which supplanted the Roman City.

We do not know much about St. Alban. The stories told
of him are legendary, but there can be little doubt that a
man of this name existed and was slain for his faith outside
Verulamium. The central fact stands, though all else may
fall.

The legendary story is told by Bede, writing in the early
eighth century. Where he got his account is not known, "but
the continuity of tradition which it reveals must surely imply
a continuity of occupation from Romano-British to Anglo-
Saxon times". (Review of *Place Names of Hertfordshire*, Transactions of the St. Albans Architectural and Archaeological
Society, 1938.) Bede tells how Alban received into his house
in Verulam a priest fleeing from persecution. He was converted by his guest. When this news became known officials
were sent to search the house. Alban sent his visitor away
and disguised himself in the priest's cloak. He was brought
before the judge, who demanded that he should perform a
ceremonial act of worship of the Roman deities. On his
refusal, Alban was tortured and then led to execution. As
was the custom the place of execution was outside the city
and Bede describes, with a remarkable topographical accuracy,
the scene when Alban was led across the River Ver by the
ford, which still exists at St. Michael's, and how the river
dried up under his feet, and how the bridge collapsed under

the press of the watching crowd. He then tells how Alban climbed the gentle hill half a mile away—a hill which we all know as we stroll up Fishpool Street to the Abbey, the hill where now the Abbey stands—and how he was beheaded. The date usually given is A.D. 303, during the persecution under Diocletian, but scholars now place the date at 209, in the persecution under Geta. Bede goes on :

"Nigh unto the city of Verulamium (which is now of the English called Verlamcaester) where after the settled calm of Christian times returned, there was a church builded of a marvellous rich work and worthy of such a martyrdom, in the which truly even unto this day are sick persons cured and doing of manifold mighty works ceaseth not to be openly wrought."

Thus it appears that the tomb of St. Alban was being reverenced long before Bede's day. In the year 429, only a hundred and twenty-six years after the traditional date of the martyrdom, the church was visited by a foreign bishop, Germanus of Auxerre, who had come to this country to refute the Pelagian heresy. He is said to have opened the tomb of Alban. As a sidelight on the condition of Verulam at the time we are told that a fire broke out in the city and did great damage because the roofs were covered with reed-thatch. The Roman roof-tiling had clearly gone. Gildas, writing in 564, is another writer who states that a church had been erected in honour of Alban and thus adds to the weight of evidence as to the essential truth of the martyrdom. In fact, between the date 209 and the arrival of Germanus, sufficient time had not elapsed for a completely false tradition to have grown up, since physical facts made it possible for people to be present at that service in 429 whose great-great-great-grandparents had actually seen Alban executed. In years to come one of the Saxon abbots was to found a chapel in honour of St. German himself, and the last ruins of that building were to be seen in Bell meadow up to the early part of the eighteenth century, when they were demolished by Admiral Killegrew, who lived at St. Julian's, not far away. The name was preserved by St. German's Farm, the site of part of which is covered by the Verulamium Museum.

According to Matthew Paris, King Offa of Mercia, in the

year 793, founded a monastery in honour of St. Alban. Though
the book on the Abbey building, published by the Historical
Monuments Commission, says that the evidence for this is
slender and some of it forged, it agrees that there was a double
monastery for men and women in being in Offa's day. There
is also some reason for believing that Offa was specially
interested in the saint, since his palace chapel in Wood Street,
London, was dedicated to St. Alban, as was the church which
later stood on that site.

What Offa did, if he had any hand in the foundation of
the monastery, was to take the existing church and perhaps
rebuild it, establishing a service of regulars to attend the
shrine and carry on divine service there. This would merely
be reinforcing a custom which was obviously already in being.
For it is clear that in the time of Bede the site of Alban's
martyrdom had become a place of pilgrimage, and therefore
there must have been a body of priests in charge to guide
pilgrims—and to accept fees and gifts. In other words, the
monastery was already in existence. There is, therefore,
nothing unlikely in the story of Offa's munificence, though
the charters quoted by Matthew Paris are, by diplomatic
evidence, forgeries.

The result of this development of the shrine as an object
of pilgrimage was that decaying Verulam was more or less
deserted, and a new settlement arose around the hill on which
the church stood. It must be remembered that, between the
erection of the first church and the days of Offa, the countryside had become Saxon. Exactly when and how this happened
and what became of the Romano-British inhabitants of
Verulamium it is impossible to say, but probably they inter-
mingled with the newcomers, inter-married, and were absorbed
and lost to history, but they brought their Christianity with
them, even though the town-dwelling tradition of the Roman
world died temporarily and gave place to the village-dwelling
tastes of the Saxons.

The British Christian girls must have converted their
Saxon husbands and all the evidence indicates that there was
no break in worship on the site which makes it probably the
earliest existing Christian site in the country still in use.

The local population inclined in an age of dangers to

cluster round some powerful organisation, be it a noble with
his private army and stronghold, or a religious house with the
spiritual powers behind it.   In the case of St. Albans it was
the protecting power of the holy saint which hastened the
final desertion of the ruins of Verulam by respectable elements,
for the Roman city was, despite the presence of Christianity
there for years, thought of as a heathen city, and super-
stitiously feared by the ignorant Saxon peasantry.

The newly constituted monastery was put under the Rule
of St. Benedict, and it remained Benedictine until the Dissolution in 1539. The Rule ordained that the monks should take
three vows : poverty, chastity and obedience. As a duty to
God and man they were enjoined to do manual work for
seven hours a day, and no doubt early monasteries really
observed this obligation, but even before the Conquest the
Benedictines were becoming renowned for learning, and the
observance of the order to do manual labour was gradually
relaxed in favour of intellectual studies until, long before the
monasteries were closed, the manual work of a religious house
and its property was being done by lay-brothers and paid
servants.

Not a great deal is known about the early Saxon abbots.
The only account we have is from Matthew Paris, writing in
the thirteenth century, and we do not know where he got
his information. We may assume that it had some basis in
fact, for he repeats scandals which, for the honour of the
Abbey, he would certainly not have invented. He tells us
that the first abbot was a kinsman of Offa, and that he is
said to have died of grief when Offa died and his son would
not let him be buried in the Abbey. The second abbot is
also said to have been related to Offa. If Matthew Paris is
to be believed, he had an exciting time, with insubordination
within and attempts at spoliation without. There is nothing
unlikely in this alleged royal kinship of the early abbots. It
was a very usual custom when a king or great noble founded
or greatly endowed a monastery or nunnery for him to
nominate a son or daughter of his house to become the ruler
of the community.

The third abbot, Wulsig, was not apparently a credit to
any religious house. Paris says, "He hunted too much and

prayed too little", but this comment is mild if one believes what is said about his character, which included a too great liking for feminine company and an extravagance which led to his selling some of the Abbey treasures. The story that the monks finally poisoned him sounds like a genuine tradition, which we cannot believe Paris invented.

The fourth abbot, Wulnoth, certainly did not have a happy time. The Abbey was attacked by the Danes. It had not been plundered before and the attack was a rude shock. In connection with this event a most remarkable story is told. The Danes, so the story goes, broke open the shrine of St. Alban and bore off the bones to Denmark, where they were placed in a shrine in a church in Odense which they dedicated to St. Alban. To this day the cathedral at Odense is so dedicated, and the authorities there claim that they still have the bones of the saint. In fact, when a party of the St. Albans City Council visited Odense in 1961 they were shown some bones which were said to be the bones of our saint.

Of course we do not agree that this is so. The monks of St. Albans were not taking this theft lying down. The Sacrist and another monk left England and, travelling as wandering monks, a familiar sight in the period, arrived at Odense and stayed there long enough to make plans for the recovery of the relics. The mission succeeded and they returned to this country in triumph, though the Danish monks always maintained that they had foiled the efforts of the English monks, and that the latter had taken away bones which were not the genuine articles. The story, in course of time, was forgotten here, though not in Denmark, but was told to Matthew Paris by some high-ranking Danish officials in the service of the King of Denmark, who had originally been either born or educated in St. Albans. They were Odo, royal treasurer to the King of Denmark ; Master John of St. Albans, known as "the Incomparable Goldsmith" ; Nicholas of St. Albans, his son, who was the king's moneyer and later became moneyer to Henry III ; and Edward the Clerk, Privy Councillor to Henry III.

Is the story true or false? Matthew Paris admits that he had never heard of it, but that it was said to be well known in Denmark. There was obviously some very early connection between St. Albans and Odense in view of the dedication of the cathedral, for Alban is not often found as the patron saint of Continental churches except in the Rhone valley. There is, of course, nothing inherently impossible in the tale, and one distinguished historian, Claude Jenkins (*The Monastic Chronicler and the Early School of St. Albans*), believes the story to be founded on fact. But if it be true, then as Rushbrooke Williams says (*History of the Abbey of St. Albans*), it constitutes a rather remarkable illustration of tenth-century monastic manners.

Ulsinus, the sixth Abbot, was, according to tradition, our first town-planner. Matthew Paris tells us that in 948 he founded three churches which dominated the entrances to the town : St. Peter's to the north, St. Stephen's to the south, and St. Michael's to the north-west, the two latter being on the Watling Street, with St. Michael's in the middle of the ruins of Verulam on the site of the Forum. He built houses at his own expense, helping settlers with money and materials. He might be called the ancestor of the modern housing committee and the plans committee of the City Council. He also founded the market which is held every Saturday to the present day in the heart of the city. When it began the Market-place was not the narrow street it is today. It stretched from French Row on the west to Chequer Street on the east. The buildings now forming streets between these two are mediaeval encroachments. Originally the great open space would be filled with stalls on market day, but by degrees there would arise a desire among traders to have permanent storage space, and then permanent living space where their stalls had stood, and rows of houses and shops filled up the market place. The small alleyways to be seen today, Queen's Way, Sovereign Way, and the rest, are the last remnants of the passages between the stalls such as may be seen on the market square every Saturday. When Ulsinus died the main lines of the modern city had been laid out. Tradition says that he also founded the school, but no authority for this is known, though Dr. F. M. L. Thompson (*St. Albans School in the Abbey*, *Abbey Papers*, *No. 2*) thinks that the fact that the master was secular and not a monk may indicate that it may, in fact, date even from before the establishment of the Benedictine Rule.

The little town suffered from the proximity of Kingsbury.

In many parts of Western Europe fortified enclosures were built up in the ninth and tenth centuries to serve as refuges from the marauding Northmen for the people of the neighbourhood. Alfred the Great founded a number of these military posts, which in some cases turned into little royal boroughs, with an official in charge. Such a one, from its name, was Kingsbury (or King's borough), which stood on top of a hill to the north-west of St. Albans. The inhabitants largely lived on the revenue of the great royal fishpond, which stretched from the ford at St. Michael's to Holywell Bridge, and the royal official was said to have oppressed the citizens of St. Albans in the days of Ulsinus. For many years there was keen rivalry between the Abbey and Kingsbury, and we may picture the Abbot and the royal official glaring at each other from their respective hilltops across the valley between, and later abbots set to work to destroy Kingsbury. Abbot Alfric bought the fishpool from Edgar the Peaceable for a large sum and drained most of it, on the pretext that it was unhealthy for his monks as it flowed just below the Abbey walls. Fishpool Street was laid out on the line of the path that skirted the mound of Kingsbury alongside the pool and was often subject to floods. One portion only of the fishpool was preserved to become the stews of the monastery, and that still remains as the lake in the gardens of St. Michael's Manor House.

The burghers of Kingsbury were in this wise deprived of their livelihood and some of them migrated to St. Albans, swelling the population, no doubt to the satisfaction of the Abbot, while the bad characters fled to the ruins of Verulam and lived there, preying on travellers, since Watling Street, the main road to the north-west, still passed through the heart of the Roman city. One of the abbots dealt with this as far as he could by closing up the end of Watling Street near St. Stephen's Church and forcing travellers to turn up Holywell Hill and pass through the town. By this he killed two birds with one stone, since the diversion brought trade to the townsmen. It is ironical to reflect that in the tenth century the town's chief citizen spent time and thought in bringing traffic into the town, while we, in our day, have to spend a lot of money in constructing roads intended to keep it out!

When the fishpool was drained a large ship is said to have been found, and an anchor. Clearly, in Roman times the Ver was big enough for vessels of some size to get up to some wharf at the foot of the wall. There was a wharf at the Roman villa at Park Street, and probably quite an amount of merchandise could be brought by water.

A still later abbot obtained permission from Canute to pull down the buildings on Kingsbury Hill, all except one, which the king decreed must be left there as a sign of royal ownership. This remained standing until the reign of Stephen, when the Abbot took advantage of a visit by the king to gain permission to clear the site completely. Henceforward the Abbot was undisputed master of the district.

A number of abbots set out to destroy the remains of Verulam in order to do away with this Alsatia, filled with all the local riffraff and bad characters. As practical men they realised the value of the building materials to be had there, and Eadmer, the eighth abbot, filled up the underground passages and began the demolition of the remains, proposing to use the building materials to rebuild the Abbey. He died before he could carry out his purpose and the piles of Roman bricks remained until the Norman abbot, Paul de Caen, pulled down the Saxon Abbey and found to his hand building materials already collected for him. The result is seen in the Abbey tower and transepts today.

It is tragic to realise the treasures of Roman culture which were lost to us by this wholesale destruction by persons completely ignorant of archaeology. Matthew Paris, in his *Lives of the Abbots*, gives us just a glimpse. He says of Eadmer :

"His pioneers overthrew the foundations of a palace in the middle of the old city ; and in the hollow place of a wall as it were in a little closet, books were found, covered with oaken boards, and silken strings fixed to, whereof one contained the life of St. Alban written in the British tongue, the rest the ceremonies of the heathen ; and when they delved into the ground, they found old tables of stone, tiles, pillars, pitchers, pots of earth and vessels of glass, containing the ashes of the dead."

The description of the finds is so like what one would expect in a "dig" today that the account seems authentic. How long did those books survive? Were they among the treasures of the great library which was scattered at the Dissolution?

We have considerable evidence from charters for the events of the reigns of the later Saxon abbots. Among them was Alfric, who was a very distinguished scholar, the son of the Earl of Kent, later to become Archbishop of Canterbury. St. Albans, up to the Dissolution, was an aristocratic Abbey, and its abbots were personal friends of royalty. Alfric's successor was his brother Leofric, who ruled the Abbey for a very long time, up to the reign of Edward the Confessor. It was he who got permission from Canute to pull down Kingsbury. During his rule the bones of St. Alban underwent another curious adventure, which is well authenticated.

The story goes that there was a scare that the Danes were threatening to invade the country again, and Leofric, fearing for the safety of the relics, wrote to the monks of Ely asking them to give the saint sanctuary until the danger was over. Ely was one of the safest places in the country, situated as it was in the heart of the Fen country and unapproachable except by paths known only to the Fen folk. Hereward the Wake, in the reign of the Conqueror, was able to hold out there for a long time, and would never have been taken but for treachery. So Leofric had good reason to believe that the bones of St. Alban would be safe there. But yet he had his doubts about the honesty of the monks of Ely. Having once got hold of the bones, would they give them up again? So he sent some anonymous bones to Ely and hid the real ones in a hole in the wall of the church. When the danger was over he sent for the bones, but the monks of Ely sent others. The abbot realised this, as he had prudently set a mark upon the ones he had sent, so he said nothing but took the genuine bones from their hiding-place and set them out in public again. But the monks of Ely, shameless in their fraud, asserted that they had the real bones of the saint, and this started one of the most famous lawsuits of the Middle Ages, one which lasted for a hundred years, and was only concluded when the English Pope, Adrian IV, the erstwhile St. Albans schoolboy, Nicholas Breakspeare, forced the monks of Ely to confess and apologise. The tale is an amazing one, and if there were not so much evidence for it, one could hardly believe that men

supposedly devoted to the service of divine truth could act
with such blatant dishonesty.

Leofric's successor was Leofstan, intimate friend of Edward
the Confessor. Chauncy says, with how much truth we do
not know, that he was related to the king. The Abbey was
steadily growing in reputation, and pilgrims were arriving in
such numbers at the shrine that men of ill-repute began to
prey on them as they travelled to the town. In order to
protect them and other travellers, Leofstan had thickets of
woodland by the wayside cut down and bridges repaired.
He gave the manor of Flamstead, near Redbourn, to a Saxon
thane named Thurnoth and two of his followers, on condition
that they should "Keep all travellers through that western
road safe from the harm of thieves and beasts who greatly
infest those parts and if any traveller should suffer by them,
that they should answer for the damage . . . and they did
perform the same until King William conquered this island
when he . . . gave it to Roger di Thoni, who willed that right
should be done to St. Alban, and this service should be strictly
performed". (Chauncy, quoting Matthew Paris.)

The last Saxon abbot was Fritheric or Frederick, who was
appointed only in 1066 and was a personal friend of Harold.
He also is said to have been of blood royal and a relation of
Canute. He was a bold man, and of him a story is told which
unfortunately is unlikely to be true, of how he stood up to
William the Conqueror at Berkhamsted, and made him take
an oath, on the relics of St. Alban, that he would maintain
the ancient laws of the realm. However this may be, William
had no liking for him, and seized the manor of Redbourn
and other property of the Abbey, and Fritheric fled to Ely,
where he died.

William would have pulled down the Abbey, but Lanfranc,
the new Archbishop of Canterbury, wanted it for his kinsman,
Paul de Caen, and as this cleric was a friend of the Conqueror
the Abbey was spared. When *Domesday Book* was compiled
it recorded the condition of St. Albans at the beginning of
the Norman period. The inhabitants were forty-six burgesses,
four Frenchmen, thirteen cottagers, and sixteen serfs tied to
the land. The total population must have been about four
hundred and sixty. The income was eleven pounds fourteen

shillings yearly, with the rents of three mills worth forty shillings yearly and the woodlands, where seven thousand pigs roamed, were worth forty shillings more. The whole rents due to the Abbey amounted to twenty pounds, having appreciated in value from twelve pounds, its value in the days of Edward the Confessor. A deer park and a fishpond are mentioned. The number of pigs is interesting, as showing how much woodland was still uncleared round St. Albans. And who were those Frenchmen?

Staircase to the Watching Gallery, in the Saint's Chapel, St. Albans Abbey.

CHAPTER THREE

THE NORMAN ABBOTS

WITH the appointment of Paul de Caen in 1077, a new chapter in the history of St. Albans and its Abbey began. It was a difficult position for the new abbot, and he had to be extremely tactful. The discipline of the monks, like that of other religious houses of Saxon England, was very lax, and one of his first tasks was to reform the Abbey. He revised the regulations and enforced them, but introduced them cautiously and gradually. One sample of his tact is shown by the fact that he induced them to relinquish their Saxon love of meat by introducing them to the French cooking of fish, which the monks found quite delicious, compensating them for the loss of their cuts off the joint. He founded the library and the scriptorium, which later became so famous, with the help of a Norman knight, Robert, who gave him two-thirds of the revenue of the manor of Hatfield to help pay for the copying of books. Lanfranc himself gave the Abbey library the enormous number of a hundred books, fifty of which were still there in the fourteenth century. Discipline at services was tightened up, and a lantern was carried round at night services so that sleepy monks, if not kept awake by the new-type music, could be seen and prodded awake. The Abbey became a model of good government, and its reputation grew so much that candidates flocked to its doors seeking admission to the ranks of the monks.

But the buildings were not on a par with the holiness of the Abbey, and Paul decided to pull down the poverty-stricken, shabby structure of the predecessors, whom Paul, with his usual courtesy slipping for once, called "*rudes et idiotas*". The only decent buildings were the buttery and the bakehouse. Paul found plenty of building material to hand, the tiles and bricks of Verulam collected by Eadmer, who had had the same idea of reconstruction. The new buildings went up quickly, though one wonders what the monks did while their home was in the hands of the builders in such a drastic fashion, but though it must have been finished long before, the Abbey was not reconsecrated until 1116. The only materials of the old building which appear to have been re-used were some balusters, probably from the church of Offa, which were set in the triforium and remain there to this day.

The Abbey soon began to acquire property outside the area. A cell was set up at Tynemouth in Northumberland on land given by Robert Mowbray, Earl of Northumberland, who became a monk at St. Albans and is buried near the high altar. Other daughter-houses acquired by the Abbey during the reign of Paul were Wallingford, Belvoir, Binham and Hertford, and under his successor, Richard d'Essai, were added Wymondham in Norfolk, and Hatfield Peverel in Essex. Even as late as 1448 this process of acquisition was still going on, for Humphrey, Duke of Gloucester, made a grant of the Priory of Pembroke in Wales to the Abbey, though a few years later the Earl of Pembroke appealed to Parliament to grant the Priory to him. Fortunately for St. Albans, a certain John Skelton got a clause inserted into the Act which safeguarded the Abbey interests. This Skelton had been an esquire of the duke, and one wonders if he were an ancestor of the Skelton who founded a charity in St. Albans many years later.

Chapters were held every year on the eve of St. Alban, at which all the priors had to be present. Occasionally an abbot would hold a visitation, though he had to get royal permission to go as far as Tynemouth. More than one abbot used this duty as a strategic excuse to leave the monastery for a period of a year or more, when the burden of hospitality grew too great for the Abbey finances.

The dependent cells were used partly for settlement and expansion of the Abbey, partly for giving the monks a holiday, and partly for punishment of unruly monks, who could thus be banished far away from their homes and friends. Some of the Abbey lands during the disorders of the Conquest had become alienated by powerful nobles, and Paul fought such men as Odo of Bayeux, the King's brother, for lands they had taken without right. In this way he recovered Tewin, Napsbury, Eywood and Redbourn, though he himself gave away lands which were not his to give, including Northaw and Sarratt, and there was trouble later in getting them back. He was not the only abbot to offend in this way, as will be seen when we consider the history of Gorhambury. On the death of Lanfranc, Paul became a good friend to Anselm, and when William Rufus withheld the revenues of Canterbury from the new archbishop, Paul lent Anselm money with which to carry on. The archbishop was grateful and was friendly towards the house.

The new Abbey building was rededicated in 1116 in the presence of a most brilliant assembly. Henry I was there with his Queen, Matilda, and his son, the Prince William, who was to lose his life when the White Ship sank. There were great nobles like Stephen of Mortain, nephew of the king (later King Stephen), and William de Warenne, besides great ecclesiastics of this country and the Continent, such as the Archbishop of Rouen. It speaks well for the healthy condition of the Abbey finances that, despite the tremendous cost of rebuilding, the revenues stood up to the strain of eleven days' splendid entertainment. The annual income about that time was in the region of £270, a very respectable sum, though not as great as that of some other religious houses.

It is under this abbot, Richard d'Essai, that we get the first definite reference to the School, still a prominent feature of the life of the modern city. Whether or not it had been founded in Saxon times, it was already well known by early Norman days, even on the Continent. It was never a monastery school, in the sense that it trained young novices for the service of the Church. There must have been a novice school in the Abbey itself as a matter of course. The pupils of the School were sons of the lesser gentry, local freemen and citizens of the town. Some even came from far away from the neighbourhood, and thus had to lodge in the town. Some of these were taken in by the Abbot, who acted towards them as a great noble acted to the young nobles he took into his household for training in knightly ways. Fees were charged to all scholars, except a few for whom a form of scholarship was provided by the Abbot, who must have occupied much the same position as chairman of the governors in a modern school. The headmaster was never a monk, though of course, like all scholars of mediaeval times, he was a cleric of some sort.

During the early years of the twelfth century the head-mastership fell vacant. How such vacancies were advertised in those days is not known, but the news reached the ears of a well-known French scholar named Geoffrey de Gorham. He decided to apply for the vacancy, but he experienced extremely bad weather in the Channel and was delayed for so long that by the time he arrived someone else had been appointed. Having made friends with the Prior (a sort of deputy abbot), he obtained a similar post at Dunstable. He was a remarkably up-to-date teacher, believing in a thoroughly modern way in the dramatic method of teaching. He wrote a play on the life of St. Catherine of Alexandria, who seems to have been his favourite saint, for his boys to perform. This is said to be the first reference to drama in English history. Wishing the scholars to dress up for the performance, he wrote to his friend the Prior of St. Albans, and borrowed from the Abbey the ceremonial copes worn by the monks on special occasions. The value of these copes can be estimated from the fact that one of the later abbots, wishing to do a deal in real estate for which he had not the ready cash, had the copes of the monks burnt to collect the gold and silver from their material. Largely from the proceeds he was able to complete his deal, and made such a good profit that he had even more gorgeous copes made to replace the ones he had destroyed.

Since copes were of such value the dismay of Geoffrey can be imagined when, after the performance, the copes which had been taken to his house were destroyed in the night when his house was burnt down. Filled with remorse, he threw up his post at Dunstable, and, coming to St. Albans, prostrated himself at the feet of the Abbot and begged to be taken in as a monk, so that he might devote the rest of his life to repairing the injury he had done the saint. The sequel was that some years later he was unanimously elected Abbot on the death of Richard in 1119.

Abbot Geoffrey founded the leper hospital of St. Julian and is reputed to have founded Sopwell for nuns, but this house is probably earlier in foundation, as his name is given as a witness to a gift of land to the cell, which had been rebuilt

by Roger the Hermit, who is buried in the south aisle of the
Abbey. Geoffrey also founded Markyate cell.

He gave great encouragement to the work of the scriptorium, and beautified the Abbey by having a costly feretory
(the box which held the relics of the saint) made by the gifted
metal worker, Anketil, an Englishman trained in Denmark,
who had become a monk in the Abbey. He was famous for
his gold and silver work, and had once been moneyer to the
King of Denmark. It is interesting to speculate how this
distinguished artist-craftsman found his way to St. Albans in
the first place, but the Abbey was known in the Middle Ages
for its gold and silver work, done in the house by artists,
some of whom became monks, while others moved on from
one religious house to another, doing work for each. When
the bones of St. Alban were transferred to Anketil's new
casket they were exhibited to a large and important audience.
We are told that the skull bore a label with the words SANCTUS
ALBANUS inscribed on it. This, according to the *Gesta Abbatum*
(the Acts of the Abbots), brought confusion to the monks of
Odense and Ely, who both now claimed to be possessors of
the true bones.

The Empress Matilda, daughter of Henry I, stayed in the
Abbey after the defeat of her cousin and rival, Stephen, at
the Battle of Lincoln in 1141, queens being the only women
permitted to pass the night within the walls. There was a
special queens' lodging later provided for them. She was
received with rejoicing, and met a deputation from London
to arrange terms. Two years later, Stephen, again on top,
was informed that the Sheriff of Hertfordshire, Geoffrey de
Mandeville, was negotiating with her, and sent a force to
arrest him at St. Albans where he was staying. Each abbey
had some knights who held land of the Abbot on the condition of rendering military service for him when necessary,
and the St. Albans' knights, considering that this move was a
violation of sanctuary, took up arms, and in the struggle the
Earl of Arundel was thrown from his horse and nearly drowned
in the Ver, which must have been somewhat deeper than it is
today; nowadays, the worst that could happen would be
wet feet! However, Geoffrey was captured and taken to
London as a prisoner.

B

When Geoffrey de Gorham became abbot, it is probable that a number of his relations followed him across the Channel, for two of his nephews became monks under him, and one of them, Robert, was promoted to the position of prior, and later on became abbot, as his uncle had been. Apparently he did not gain these honours because of his relationship to Geoffrey, for they came to him after his uncle's death. Family affection, however, led Geoffrey to do the community a wrong which was to make trouble and cost a good deal of money to a successor two hundred years later. He gave the manor of Westwick to a kinsman, who built himself a house which he called Gorhambury. When, in 1957, a group of local archaeologists started an excavation to find the remains of this house, they discovered that its foundations were mixed with the foundations of a Roman villa, so that it would appear that de Gorham built on the remains of Roman structure. The presence of Roman tiles and bricks probably suggested the site of the new house to a thrifty Frenchman.

It was Geoffrey's successor who burnt the copes of the monks to get the precious metal out of them, and he was vandal enough to strip the shrine of the metalwork to be melted down. One must add that he carefully omitted to include his own plate in the destruction, and, to do him justice, that he replaced the metalwork on the shrine with still more beautiful work. As Anketil was still alive, one wonders just what he thought of this treatment of his work, and whether he did any of the new metalwork. This particular abbot was a good financier, and had the foresight to start a fund for the upkeep of the fabric of the Abbey.

For years a rivalry had existed between the Abbots of St. Albans and Westminster for the precedence among abbots. The Abbot of Westminster claimed that he must take precedence of all the rest because the king was crowned in his abbey; the Abbot of St. Albans countered with the claims of the first British martyr. On occasion the rival abbots descended to jostling each other in the doorway of the Great Council in the effort to be the one to go in first. The matter was settled in the time of Robert de Gorham. There was, in the Abbey, a monk named Breakspear, whose family were tenants of the Abbey at Abbot's Langley. He had been accepted after the death of his wife on proving that he was a good living man, and that his education was adequate. His son, Nicholas, who must have been educated at the school, since the headmaster had the monopoly of education in the area, and was a kind of local education authority on his own, also wished to enter the Abbey, but after examination was failed as not being up to standard. He went abroad, and finally to Rome, where he ended up as Pope Adrian IV, the only Englishman who has ever been Pope. He bore no grudge against the Abbey; on the contrary, he evidently had a soft corner in his heart for it, and when Robert de Gorham made his official visit to Rome on appointment, the Pope gave some very valuable privileges to the Abbey. They included freedom from the jurisdiction of any bishop and from the visitation of any but a papal legate. The question of precedence was settled in favour of St. Albans, and remained with it, except for some occasional successes of Westminster, until not long before the Dissolution. The Abbot was given the privilege which all abbots yearned for, that of wearing mitre and full canonicals when celebrating Mass. What those canonicals were can be seen in the beautiful brass of Abbot Thomas de la Mare, which is one of the glories of the Abbey today.

All this time the reputation of the Abbey was growing, and one monk was elected Abbot of Selby, another Abbot of Crowland, and a third Abbot of Westminster itself. At the Council of Tours, Robert proudly took precedence of all the English abbots present, and at home he received an elaborate grant of liberties from Henry II, a most comprehensive document which conferred on the Abbey "all liberties which kingly power can bestow on any church". It was confirmed by a number of kings as time went on, and in the reign of Henry IV was repeated in more exact language.

Fortunately for Robert, who was no financier, and left the Abbey in debt, the officer known as the cellarer, who might be called the steward of the house, like the bursar of a college, was an able business man. His name was Adam, and when Robert died the king left the administration in his hands. He was so successful in extricating the Abbey from its difficulties that when he died he was buried among the abbots as if he had been one himself. As a hobby he drew up a *Rotulus* of happenings in his lifetime, and this was later drawn on by Matthew Paris, and may be regarded as the germ from which grew the school of history for which St. Albans became famous. There is a portrait of Adam in the St. Albans Book of Benefactors, showing him with a purse in one hand and a key in the other.

A Statue of St. Alban on the Screen behind the High Altar,
St. Albans Abbey.

CHAPTER FOUR

LIFE IN THE ABBEY IN THE EARLY MIDDLE AGES

IT may be convenient at this point to give an account of the Abbey and its life at this time. The monastery owned St. Albans and the surrounding lands from Codicote to Rickmansworth, and from Abbot's Langley to Barnet and Northaw. It also owned Hexton and Newnham in the north of the county, and many estates in Bedfordshire and Buckinghamshire. It had outlying cells in Norfolk and at Wallingford, and as far north as Tynemouth in Northumberland. St. Albans was governed by a reeve appointed by the Abbot, and he collected tolls and dues and carried out the Abbot's orders. A borough court met once a year. For summary jurisdiction the tenants went to the Court of the Ashtree, held nominally under a great ash tree in the courtyard of the monastery, but having regard to our climate it was probably usually held in some courtroom of the Abbey. In the later Middle Ages this was most likely the Moot Hall, now occupied by Messrs. W. H. Smith's bookshop. This court was supposed to be held every three weeks, but as in other manors elsewhere in the country, it no doubt varied and was held when there was business to transact. The burgesses, as trade grew, became properous, and the more prosperous they grew the more they hated the jurisdiction of the Abbey. On the lands around the town there were many customary tenants who were bound to pay various dues to the monastery —"weekwork", which was a certain number of hours' work on the monastery land every week; "boonwork", which was work due at certain seasons, such as harvest and ploughing; "heriot" which in most parts of the country was a payment of the best beast in the possession of the tenant at his death, but to which at St. Albans was added the cruel demand for all the household furniture. Probably this was returned to the widow or heir, but as a favour, and it was unusually severe. They also had to pay "merchet"—a payment to be permitted to marry—and a number of other payments which became increasingly irksome as time went on. And, of course, customary tenants could be prevented from leaving the estate, or, if given permission, they had to pay "chevage" or "head-money" annually, as compensation for the loss of their services.

It is difficult to estimate the revenue produced by pilgrims. The income of the Abbey was divided among departments, and it was run like a big business. The Abbot did not live with his monks, but had his own private residence where he entertained royalty and great nobles, though on occasion he would dine them in state on the dais in the refectory. The departmental heads were as follows:

1. The Seneschal or Steward, often a layman of high rank, was responsible for the secular interests of the Abbey. When the Abbot went to law, which was an occupational hobby among quite a number, the seneschal acted as the Abbot's attorney and represented him in the royal courts.

2. The Prior was deputy abbot and had apartments of his own.

3. The Precentor was responsible for the services in the church. He was choirmaster and librarian.

4. The Cellarer had care of everything relating to the provision of food and accommodation, and had horses and servants and often an apartment of his own. He had a number of sub-officers in his department, and needed great organising ability. One might call him the managing director.

5. The Sacristan had care of the fabric and furniture of the church, and looked after the ornaments and relics and jewels. Sometimes he slept in a chamber built in the church itself.

6. The Hospitaller or Guestmaster was responsible for guests. Travellers were received for a day and a night, and as St. Albans was just one day's journey from London, and all travellers who came through the town had to stop there before continuing their journey, the guestmaster was kept busy, because, though many of the travellers were traders, business men and so on, and they put up at the very numerous inns and hostels in the town, many were official visitors and had to be accommodated in or near the Abbey, and the pilgrims also had to be catered for. So there were several guesthouses to be provided. The biggest was on the corner of Spicer

Street and George Street (then known as Church Lane), and the guestmaster's office was in Chequer Street. Important visitors might stay in the Abbey itself, and the whole business of providing for them imposed a very great strain on the finances of the monastery, so much so that on occasion the Abbey was on the verge of bankruptcy, for though visitors were expected to leave some gift which should go towards covering their expenses, quite frequently they omitted to do so, or at least adequately. The Abbey provided stabling for three hundred horses in the Long Stabling along the western side of Abbey Mill Lane.

7. The Infirmarer looked after the sick quarters, which provided not only for sick monks but also for other sick and wounded. He was assisted by a physician and servants, and was supposed to organise visits to sufferers outside the Abbey.

8. The Kitchener was responsible for the actual provision of food, and had a staff of cooks and kitchen helps. He was the housekeeper and went to market with his pack animals, sometimes as far as London, to bring back provisions, which were unloaded by the tradesmen's entrance, the Sumpter Yard (sumpter means a pack animal).

9. Other officials were the Almoner, responsible for the charity of the house, the Chamberlain, and the officer responsible for the running of the refectory. In addition, there were hosts of sub-officers in all departments.

All these officials had certain revenues earmarked for their departments. An echo of this is the name of a house in Fishpool Street, Kitchener's Meads. The rents of these water meadows went to supply the expenses of the cook's department. Spicer Street reminds us of one of the minor officials who were attached to the kitchener's staff, and the spicer had an office alongside that of the guestmaster in Chequer Street. Childwick was a dairy farm which provided milk for the young monks— the "children".

In 1194 the Abbot assigned one mark (13s/4d) of the tithes of Abbot's Walden (now St. Paul's Walden) towards the maintenance of a chaplain at the leper hospital of the Pré which he had founded. A later vicar of Walden had to pay forty shillings a year for the supply of bread for the monks' guesthouse at St. Albans, and later still all the tithes of Walden were appropriated to the official in charge of the refectory, though by 1500 part was diverted to the hospital of St. Julian's, which also had fifty shillings paid by the kitchener. Surrounding estates had to pay towards the Abbey finance, and this is probably the origin of Cell Barnes at St. Albans and Sell Barnes at King's Walden. These were not manor houses for monks, but halls of estates where the work of the manor was organised and rents and goods collected for transmission to the Abbey.

The Abbot had a separate income out of which he had to bear special expenses such as taxation and entertainment of important guests like royalty. If the Abbot's pocket was empty, an embarrassing situation might arise. In fact, once, when Edward II came to stay at the Abbey, the Abbot had not even enough money to buy bread for his royal guest and had to borrow from him to supply the table. Occasionally an Abbot would give generously of his spare income (when he had any) to assist the general expenses of the house. Geoffrey de Gorham gave help to the kitchen. The kitchener had thirty-three shillings a week, which covered thirty shillings for food and three shillings for the carriers who brought supplies from London. Also he had forty-eight hens and a pig at Christmas, and a thousand eggs and a pig at Easter from Rickmansworth. As expenses rose, with more inmates and rising prices, this amount did not cover the costs, so Geoffrey gave five shillings a week out of his own pocket and all the cheeses that came to him from Sandridge, Langley and Walden.

There were a large number of people living in the Abbey besides the monks, who at the height of its fame mustered seventy-seven. There were also the lay brothers, who were the servants, and tradesmen—millers, bakers, tailors, shoemakers, smiths, grooms and so on. Then there were the fraternity. Certain knights and merchants treated the monastery as a retirement home, lived there as if in an hotel, and paid for their board and lodging. They wore ordinary dress, but were buried in the monks' cemetery, and as a special favour might be buried in monk's robes. Sometimes a benefactor would stipulate that the Abbey should provide food and accommodation for some old servant of his. Kings often provided for this kind of pension, called a corrody, for their old courtiers.

The monks attended a number of services from midnight mass to vespers, though busy officials might be excused from some of them. But few could be excused from the daily meeting in the chapter house, when all Abbey business which concerned the monks was transacted, complaints were heard, and discipline enforced. Work went on between these services, and dinner was about eleven o'clock. No one was supposed to speak at dinner, except by signs, and one would have seen a number of hands waving like fishes' tails when the diners desired more fish. One of the monks read from a good book while the meal progressed. On special days, such as saints' days, a "pittance" was allowed, an extra dish. Occasionally there was a feast day, when they were treated to luxuries, but these were balanced by fast days. As discipline became less rigid later in the Middle Ages, meat was eaten at times, but not in the refectory; it was served in a special room called the *misericord* or pity room.

After dinner in summer, novices and junior monks played games in the cloister, and it would be interesting to know what games they indulged in. Ball games, of course; there are so many representations in illuminated manuscripts of people playing ball that it must have been a general pastime. Apprentices played the ancestor of football, and there was a game which looks like a cross between hockey and golf. They played skittles, a very old game, and leapfrog is shown in manuscript illustrations. So we can imagine these youngsters casting off the seriousness becoming to members of a religious community, and thoroughly enjoying themselves. Meanwhile their elders indulged in an after-dinner nap.

Then came another service, after which the monks went for a time to whatever work they did. After vespers, at five in winter and six in summer, came supper, after which they went to the chapter house for a session of listening to readings, and then had their one really free time of the day when they chatted in the cloister, or, in winter, warmed themselves in the warming-room at the only fire in the monastery. After another short service they went to bed at seven in winter and eight in summer. At midnight the whole routine started all over again.

CHAPTER FIVE

THE ABBEY IN THE TWELFTH AND
THIRTEENTH CENTURIES

SIMON, the nineteenth Abbot (1167–1183), was a gentle
soul, peaceable and a lover of learning. He started
under difficulties. Some of the snobbish monks objected
that he was born of common burgesses, and would be likely
to be vulgarly keen on money, and, indeed, certain aspects of
his career gave some colour to this criticism. But he must
have found it somewhat awkward to rule over the aristocratic
community of St. Albans.

However, he overcame his critics and was a distinguished
ruler. He attracted men of learning to the Abbey, and
regulated the scriptorium, in which he himself supported two
or three writers. He had his own special book-chest, and a
manuscript picture shows him sitting by it. He completed
the shrine of St. Alban, and some beautiful goldsmith's work
was done on it by Master John, "the incomparable goldsmith" (one of those who told the amazing story of Odense
and the Bones), but money being short the Abbot had to
borrow money from Aaron, the famous Jew of Lincoln, who,
being obviously a man with a sense of humour, boasted that
he had made possible the splendid new shrine of St. Alban
and provided the saint with a home.

When Simon made regulations for the scriptorium, he
ordained that every abbot should maintain one special writer
at his own expense. He instituted the office of historiographer,
which was held by Roger of Wendover until his death in
1236. His successor was the famous historian, Matthew Paris,
whose stupendous achievement made the scriptorium of St.
Albans so well known that great men, both English and
foreign, when they made their inevitable visit to St. Albans,
took care to talk to him, inviting him to dine with them, and
generally behaving like modern statesmen granting a press
interview. Consequently, his knowledge of home and foreign

affairs is remarkable, straight from the horse's mouth, so to speak. He travelled on the Continent, too, and he included copies of many original documents in his books of which otherwise we should know nothing, and he is indeed one of the really great men of our town. He is an example of the way in which monks of such an abbey, so far from being recluses, narrow and parochial, were men of the world, able to mix in any society. Life came to them; they had no need to leave their cloister to go in search of it.

When Paris died in 1259 he was succeeded by men only slightly less able than himself, Rishanger, Trokelowe, Walsingham and others, who carried the work up to the fifteenth century.

Simon, the gentle dove, tried to make peace between those two eagles, Henry II and Becket, which shows that he did not lack for courage, but his intervention was fruitless and Becket was murdered.

When Simon died the succession was disputed, and there was a contested election which resulted in Warin, the Prior, becoming abbot. The first thing he did was to make his brother prior and his nephew the headmaster of the school. They were a tough trio, and the Abbot did much as he liked, for his nephew was a lawyer, and his legal knowledge was at the service of his uncle. Warin alienated Abbey property to endow his new foundation of St. Mary de Pratis, or Pré, a leper hospital for women. He felled woodlands, and set up in business as a timber merchant on his own account. He relaxed the rigour of the Rule and allowed the sick brethren to go to the cell at Redbourn as a sort of convalescent home on light duty. Discipline there was so easy that, later on, the behaviour became a public scandal. He was a friend of Richard the Lionheart, who visited him at the Abbey, and was entertained at great expense. In 1193 a demand was made that all chalices in England should be given up to help pay the king's ransom when Richard was a prisoner, but the Abbot managed to save those belonging to the Abbey on payment of two hundred marks. Perhaps the expense of the king's entertainment had brought dividends.

Two years later Warin died and was succeeded by John de Cella (1195–1214), the first abbot from one of the dependent

houses, Wallingford. He was a very learned man and supported the scriptorium well. He was bitten by the same fever
which seems to be afflicting the traders of St. Albans in these
days, the desire to pull down the old buildings and rebuild
them in the latest style of "contemporary architecture". He
planned to rebuild the west front of the Abbey in Early English
style, and had it pulled down. But he was swindled by a
rascally contractor, and the money was exhausted before the
foundations were properly constructed. The unpaid workmen
decamped, and the unprotected work was damaged by our
typical weather. John lavished all his available funds on the
job, and sent a cleric round the country alleging that he had
been raised from the dead by the merits of St. Alban, and
inviting subscriptions. But evidently the public did not think
that the result had justified the effort of the saint, and the
subscriptions did not come up to expectations. Meanwhile,
he had to rebuild and extend the refectory and recondition
the dormitory. The monks themselves volunteered to give up
their wine for fifteen years. It may be significant that at the
same time he earned the approval of Matthew Paris by
making an order that the strength of the beer was to be
improved. Paris says feelingly that the beer "alike to our
damage and our disgrace was weak beyond all measure".

It was at this time that some of the paintings in the nave
were done by a very artistic family, William of Colchester,
his brother and his nephew, the first and last of whom were
monks. John de Cella was a very strict abbot, and the reputation of the Abbey for piety and learning grew so much and
there were so many candidates for entry that the Abbot had
to make a rule that the number of monks should not exceed
one hundred. As the average previously had been about
fifty, this is evidence of the high repute of the house.

John de Cella had to rule in unruly times. He had to
struggle against the powerful baron, Robert Fitzwalter, who
claimed Northaw by a forged charter, which he had managed
to get sealed with the conventual seal, through the treachery
of a discontented monk. After that the seal was more closely
guarded, and the monk was banished to Tynemouth, where
he is said to have met with such a tragic death that Robert
was scared into reconciliation with the monastery, but his

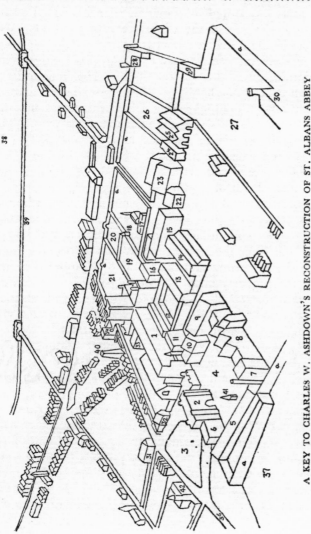

A KEY TO CHARLES W. ASHDOWN'S RECONSTRUCTION OF ST. ALBANS ABBEY

1. Abbey Church
2. Great Gateway
3. Romeland
4. Great Court
5. Long Stable
6. Seneschal's House and Almonry
7. Water Gate
8. The Long House
9. The King's Hall
10. The Guests' House
11. The Abbot's Parlour and Chapel
12. The Cloister
13. The Refectory
14. The Oriolum or Gallery
15. The Dormitories
16. Chapter House
17. Prior's House
18. Columbarium or Dove Cote
19. Monks' Cemetery
20. Sumpter Yard
21. Vineyard
22. House of the Chamberlain
23. Infirmary
24. Archdeacon's House
25. Library
26. Orchard
27. The Great Orchard
28. Holywell Gate
29. Almoner's Gate
30. Derne Gate
31. Corner Hall; the Great Guesthouse
32. Polyamdrium; the Charnel House
33. Sacrist's House
34. Waxhouse Gate
35. Vintry, now High Street
36. Fishpool Street or Salipath
37. Kitcheners Meads
38. Keyfields
39. Tonman Ditch and Boundary Wall
40. Clock Tower
41. King's Well
42. Grammar School
a Defensive Walls of Abbey

repentance was very temporary. He was patron of Binham
Priory, one of the Abbey cells, and he appointed a prior
whom the Abbot removed, to the fury of Robert, who actually
besieged Binham to compel the monks there to say that they
wanted his candidate. The Abbot appealed to King John,
who took the opportunity to seize Robert's lands and sent a
force to Binham. At the moment John was friendly to the
Abbey, but this did not last. Because of John's misdeeds
the Pope had placed England under an interdict, which meant
that the religious life of the country stopped entirely. No
services could be held, no burial services could be read,
baptisms ceased and marriages could take place only in the
church porch, not in the church itself. The king ordered
Abbot John to continue holding services, and when the Abbot
not unnaturally refused, the king seized the house into his
own hands and installed secular officials of his own. The
Abbot tried to bribe him with six hundred marks to take
them away, and when he had paid this blackmail the unfortunate Abbot was faced with a demand for another five
hundred under threat of a return of the royal officials.

Therefore the monks must have rejoiced at a most important series of events. John had been successful in alienating
all classes of the community, and both Church and barons
were suffering from the way in which he strained the royal
powers to despoil both. When a bishop or abbot died the
king took the property of the see or monastery into his own
hands, and sent royal officials to take over the administration
(and the revenues), until the vacancy was filled. By refusing
or delaying royal permission to elect, he could spin out the
time during which he received the revenues. Similarly, if a
baron died, if the heir was under age, the king became the
guardian of his lands and person until he attained his majority
(usually at the age of sixteen). During this time he could do
as he liked with the property, and arrange the marriage of
the heir to whomsoever he chose. In 1213 discontent over
these matters became acute, and the Archbishop of Canterbury,
Stephen Langton, induced the king to promise to make some
restitution to the Church. A council was summoned to meet
at St. Albans on the fourth of August, to which the barons
came as well as ecclesiastics. The Justiciar explained to the

meeting the extent of the compensation which John had agreed to, and the Archbishop started a discussion on the misgovernment of the king, and produced a charter of Henry I, giving a general idea of the liberties of freemen. This was amended and a statement drawn up, which the Archbishop presented to another meeting at St. Paul's, and this was the basis of Magna Carta. So while St. Paul's may be very proud of hearing Magna Carta read, and Bury St. Edmunds proud that there the barons accepted it, as the document to be demanded from the king, St. Albans has the distinction of having heard it first in its earliest form. That is why the Mayor of St. Albans is an *ex officio* member of the Magna Carta Trust, formed in 1955 to commemorate the granting of this important charter of liberties, a landmark in the history of Britain, the Commonwealth, the United States, and all the free world. The members are St. Albans, London, Bury St. Edmunds, Egham and Canterbury.

Magna Carta has often been called the beginning of the reign of law, but one aspect of the meeting at St. Albans has enormous significance in the history of democracy. The meeting was attended not only by bishops, abbots and barons, but also by the representative reeve and four men from every township on the royal estates. It has been called the "first historical instance of the extension to a national council of the representative machinery which had long existed in the Folkmoot of the Shire". (Taswell-Lanmead: *Constitutional History*.) In other words, it was the beginning of Parliament, and St. Albans was the scene of its inception. Indeed, we have much to be proud of.

But before the meeting at St. Paul's, John de Cella died and was succeeded by the twenty-second abbot, William de Trumpington, who was destined to have a most troublous reign. When John ignored Magna Carta and showed that he had no intention of keeping it, the barons invited the King of France who, by feudal law, was their overlord, and John's, as far as their lands in France were concerned, to take possession of England and depose John. He sent his son, the Dauphin, who in the course of his campaign occupied St. Albans in December 1217. He quartered his troops in the neighbourhood of what is now called the High Street, but then was the Vintry, and ordered the Abbot to do him homage. When the Abbot refused, he threatened to set fire to the Abbey and the town. He was pacified by the payment of eighty marks and withdrew, but the people of St. Albans were so impressed by the presence of French soldiers in their midst that they nicknamed part of the market at the back of the Flesh Shambles, French Row, a name which it keeps to this day. The first mention of the name is found in 1259; it is given without any explanation, showing that it was already established as the familiar name of the street.

But the Abbey was not yet out of its troubles. If the French had chastised the unfortunate place with whips, the army of the new little king, Henry III, under Faulkes de Breauté, chastised it with scorpions only a month later. In January, de Breauté sacked the town and demanded a hundred marks of silver to ransom the Abbey from fire. He burnt one of the citizens in the Vintry, and committed murder in the Abbey itself. Then he was seized with remorse for the violation of sanctuary and submitted to be scourged by the monks, but his repentance did not go far enough to induce him to return his ill-gotten gains. Only a few months later the Dauphin came again and despoiled St. Albans once more, before moving off to Dunstable to ravage that town. Matthew Paris says that altogether the Abbot paid out more than £2,500. This must be an exaggeration, because the total income of the House at the time was somewhere about £600. But the depredations were extremely serious, especially in livestock. In twelve months the Abbot was stated to have lost a hundred horses, and this may not be an exaggeration.

But life went on in the town. About this time (the thirteenth century), records mention conveyance of stalls in the market, and soon after, in the early fourteenth century, the term "shop" supersedes "stall", showing that the permanent buildings were taking the place of temporary ones, and Market Place and Chequer Street were taking their modern lines. And, amazingly, much rebuilding went on in the Abbey. Trumpington at last finished John de Cella's west front. The two aisles were re-roofed and re-beamed, the tower was heightened and crowned with a tall octagonal spire. The interior was beautified with fine carving, done by Walter of

Colchester, one of the talented family previously mentioned. The Abbey acquired a London house and another at Yarmouth, where salt fish might be stored, when bulk purchase seemed desirable. To raise money all sorts of expedients were resorted to. A tax was levied on the dependent houses, but while the men submitted to the demand philosophically, the nuns of St. Mary de Pratis refused flatly, complained to the Pope and had to be let off the payments. Messengers were sent off all over England on begging missions inviting subscriptions, letters were obtained from the king ordering Abbey tenants to contribute—evidently they were being obstinate in their refusal, which shows that there was a growing sense of independence among the burgesses. Then there were the offerings of pilgrims, and wealthy guests were expected to contribute to the cost of entertainment, with a little over, as a sort of tip to the saint.

Abbot Trumpington improved the discipline and withdrew some of the relaxations. He held high mass every day, and insisted on attendance at it. He presented a number of books to the library and spent a good deal of pains on the organisation of the scriptorium. It was during his reign that Roger of Wendover started the school of history. His work was called the "Flowers of History", and it was based on an earlier work. He was a good writer, careful and trustworthy. Trumpington died in 1236 and Wendover died at about the same time. Matthew Paris took over the work of official historian and his work went on until 1259.

Trumpington was succeeded by John de Hertford. He was already an old man, and was considered too frail to take the customary long journey to Rome to present himself to the Pope. But he was remarkably vigorous for his age, and ruled for twenty-eight years. Paris approvingly says of him that he did not enrich his relations, "a merit which can be ascribed with truth to none, or at any rate few of his predecessors".

Like so many abbots, he spent a good deal of money on building enterprises. He built a beautiful guest hall, with special rooms for royal guests. Towards this the king and some nobles made a contribution. He improved the buttery and its products. He found the mills very old and dilapidated and almost useless, since the Ver could no longer give sufficient strength to turn them, so he set up a horse mill near the brewery at the foot of what is now the Abbey orchard. He also pulled down the Norman apse at the east end of the Abbey church.

Lawsuits might almost be called his hobby, and he fought one action after another. One of these was against the knight who held Childwick. A recent right obtained by the Abbot was that no one should hunt on Abbey lands without permission—the right of warren, as it was called—and Geoffrey of Childwick offended the Abbot by daring to hunt on his own land. This the Abbot called "entering violently". But when the Abbot sued him, Geoffrey got a charter from the king giving him the right to hunt on his own land. The Abbot ignored this and tried force. Geoffrey countered by sueing the Abbot, who had to pay a fine of fifty marks. In the end the Abbot, realising that he had caught a tartar, made the best of a bad job and bought him out with a manor in Newbury to get rid of him.

In other disputes, John fought for and preserved threatened privileges of the Abbey, and even succeeded in adding to them. But all the time he was fighting the extortion of both king and Pope. In fact, the Papacy was so unpopular in the Abbey at this time that the chronicler relates somewhat acidly that when the papal seal with an image on it was fastened to the Abbey tower as a protection against lightning, it had no effect. Yet though the Abbey finances were hard hit the Abbot still lived as a great noble, entertaining kings and training young lads of noble birth in the ways of society. Matthew Paris reached the height of his powers and his reputation, and entered in his writing lists of the rich treasures given to the saint, as well as copies of charters which have now disappeared, and about which we should know nothing but for him. Some of the revenue came from rents in the town, and at this time we hear of a house in St. Peter's Street paying five shillings a year, and a shop on Holywell Hill two shillings.

Towards the end of Abbot John's life the country became involved in the struggle between Henry III and the barons, led by Simon de Montfort, Earl of Leicester. The Abbey, having suffered so from the demands of the king, inclined to the side of the barons, and had an immense admiration for de Montfort. In 1261 the barons summoned three knights from each shire to meet them at St. Albans. The presence of knights of the shire would have been a further step at St. Albans in the development of Parliament, but when the king heard of the summons, he issued a counter-summons to meet him at Windsor the same day, specially forbidding them to go anywhere else.

The danger of conflict caused the authorities here to improve the defences of the town, and they were so much strengthened that St. Albans was nicknamed "Little London". What these defences were is not clear. Paris says that the town was defended by gates, bolts and bars, but gates would have been of little use unless the spaces between them were defended by a wall or something of the sort. Was St. Albans walled in the Middle Ages or not? There is now no physical trace of any wall, but that is no valid argument against its existence. Many towns had walls that have not survived. As Beresford and Joseph say (*Mediaeval England: an Aerial Survey*), "Townsmen did not spend money on walls for orna- ment: in the pacific centuries when walls became unnecessary, there was no enthusiasm for their maintenance, and many have completely disappeared from view". On the other hand, there are other facts which could tend to suggest that St. Albans did have a wall. The town was more or less surrounded with a ditch, the Tonman Ditch, traces of which are still to be seen, and this may have been crowned with a timber fence, but on the map of 1700, reproduced in Chauncy's history, there is a field named Wall Close, occupying the space from the Marlborough Almshouses to the south-east, along Marlborough Road, right on the line of the Tonman Ditch. Further, the part of St. Peter's Street north of the bus station is still correctly called the Bowgate, which has, I think erroneously, been taken to be a corruption of Borough Gate. It is easier to think that it means just what it says, i.e. an arch of stone forming a gate. The word "bow" always means an arch, as at Lincoln, where the Stonebow is one of the ancient gates of the city, and Bow in London takes its name from St. Mary le Bow, St. Mary of the Arches. We have a simple little example in our own neighbourhood. On the road to Redbourn along the A5 road, the Watling Street, there is a little mediaeval bridge, sometimes called Shafford Bridge, but to all old St. Albans people it is Bow Bridge.

The Bowgate would not have kept out strangers if they could have walked round the sides of it. There were strong defences called bars at crossings on all the roads into the town, at Shropshire Lane (Victoria Street), just where Marlborough Road crosses it, at Holywell Hill near Sopwell Lane, where the road from London came into the town, and across Catherine Street by the junction of Church Street and Etna Road. Ashdown *(St. Albans: Historical and Picturesque)*, writing in 1893, states that when a field (now covered with council houses) was cut up for allotments near the eastern end of Sopwell Lane, a considerable portion of the foundations of the mediaeval wall, of large stones roughly squared with flints in mortar, was exposed to view. Unfortunately, Ashdown is not to be trusted, and he does not say that he himself saw it, but it will be seen that there is at least sufficient evidence of the presence of a wall to make the conjecture believable.

If it be so, then the line of the wall may have run roughly thus, following the line of the Tonman Ditch; from the Abbey Wall across Holywell Hill, south of Sopwell Lane, to the eastern end of that lane, up Keyfield Terrace across the modern London Road, along the line of Marlborough Road to Hatfield Road (which was then a short lane, Cock Lane, petering out into a rough track to Hatfield), behind St. Peter's Church to Bowgate, then turning sharply back (the Tonman Ditch makes a V-shaped turn there) across Grange Street to Catherine Street, down Folly Lane to the Victoria Playing Fields (whose deep hollows, since filled up, formed part of the ditch), to the New England Street playing field (originally a Roman sandpit, then a part of the defences of Kingsbury Castle, and taken into the Tonman Ditch system), along Wellclose Street to the Abbey Wall.

Roger of Norton, John's successor, continued the support of the barons against the king, and attended the Parliament of Simon de Montfort, who is highly praised by Rishanger, the chronicler who followed Matthew Paris. The town was in full agreement with the Abbey, and in 1265 the Castellan of Hertford was sent to arrest four leading burghers of the town to make them sureties for the good behaviour of the rest. He came in a spirit of incredible bravado, with only three companions, and a hostile mob attacked them and lynched them. After peace was restored the town was fined a hundred marks, and paid up willingly and easily, showing that the town was prosperous and the burgesses wealthy. But this very prosperity led to bad relations between the Abbey and its tenants. Whereas on royal estates and those of great nobles it had been quite easy to obtain charters of liberty in return for money (badly needed at the time of the Crusades, and easily found by well-to-do burghers), this was impossible on the lands of religious houses, and it was felt to be an intolerable situation that prosperous tradespeople should be subject to irritating liabilities.

As an example may be mentioned the case of the fulling-mills. The Abbot had the right to compel all townsfolk to full their cloth at his mills, and the fees from this constituted an important item in his income, but it was a constant source of trouble. In 1274 some of the burgesses set up mills of their own. The Abbot's bailiffs carried off the stones and the townspeople sued the Abbot for trespass, and some even carried the case to Westminster. But they failed in their suit and were imprisoned. Meanwhile some of the women of St. Albans had appealed to Queen Eleanor, when she came to the town, but either they were very incoherent, or she was slow of understanding, for she failed to comprehend what they were complaining about and was unable to help them. She came again to the Abbey, but as a dead woman, when her body lay in state in front of the altar on its journey to Westminster. Edward I put up an Eleanor Cross here to commemorate the event, as at other places where her body rested, and it stood in front of the Clock Tower until the seventeenth century, when the top was taken off, and the rest was destroyed about 1701, when the Mayor's accounts show an item of money paid for a room in the Christopher Yard to put the stones and rubbish from the old cross. It was replaced by an octagonal structure surmounted by a figure of Justice which contained the town pump. This building was removed in 1810.

Edward I stayed at the Abbey seven times, and it is a proof of the high esteem in which the scholarship of the monks was held that when he wanted to claim the crown of Scotland he asked the Abbey to search the records to find arguments to back up his claim.

A drawing based on the brass of Abbot Thomas de la Mare
in St. Albans Abbey.

CHAPTER SIX

SOME GREAT ABBOTS

I<small>T</small> was unfortunate for the Abbey that, at this time, the
beginning of the fourteenth century, there occurred a
succession of short-lived abbots, for John of Berkhamsted,
the twenty-fifth Abbot, had made what he considered a very
good bargain with the king, by which the king gave up the
right of taking the possessions of the Abbey during a vacancy,
but received a thousand marks at each occasion instead. This
was altogether too big a sum, and when one abbot after
another died, the effect on the Abbey finances was like recurring
death duties today. His immediate successor was weak and
almost gave in to a preposterous demand on the part of the
Bishop of Lichfield, but the monks had more backbone, and
successfully defied the bishop. The next abbot was Hugh of
Eversden, a man of the world and a cultured gentleman, a
friend of Edward II. He found the finances in such a parlous
state that he had to appoint a guardian of the gate to keep
out the bailiffs! This was the abbot who had to borrow from
the king to buy bread for the royal table.

Yet incredibly he started building operations which
culminated in the lovely Lady Chapel, but which were hope-
lessly extravagant considering the state of the exchequer, and
drained the resources dry. Then the wall of the lavatory
fell down and had to be repaired, and as misfortunes never
come singly, on a Sunday in October, 1323, five of the great
Norman pillars on the south side of the nave fell with a crash,
bringing down the roof of the south aisle, and doing terrible
damage. All this work had to be repaired, and the Abbey
lived from hand to mouth. The nave today shows clearly
where the break occurred, and the new work carried out
under Hugh can be easily distinguished.

For some years relations between the Abbey and the
townsfolk had been steadily deteriorating. The Abbey was
twice besieged by townspeople demanding liberties. Once

the mob broke into the Abbey and carried off muniments. Another time they claimed that the town was the property of the king and not of the Abbey, and that they should elect the two members who were chosen by the abbots to go to the meetings of Parliament. On the whole they wished to take over the powers of the Abbot and be independent. The Abbot was forced to accede to their demands, because his friend Edward II, whom he had openly supported, had been deposed and murdered, and power was in the hands of his enemies, Queen Isabella and the Earl of Mortimer. A royal commission was appointed to enquire into the causes of defects in the Abbey and its finances. This was a sign of changing times. Once, no government would have dared to interfere in the internal affairs of the most important Abbey in the kingdom, and this latest move shows the growing strength of the secular authority.

But the Abbey was lifted out of the doldrums by the rule of the three greatest abbots, Richard of Wallingford, Michael of Mentmore and Thomas de la Mare. The first had been a monk of the dependent house of Wallingford, and had been sent to Oxford, as had become the custom among the great abbeys, to send promising young monks to the university. Having obtained his bachelor's degree, Richard came to St. Albans, but Abbot Hugh, recognising his great capacity for learning, sent him back to get his master's degree. He was probably St. Albans' cleverest citizen before Francis Bacon. When he was elected Abbot in 1327 he found the Abbey so deeply in debt that the prospect of pulling something out of the disaster would have daunted a lesser man.

He began well. A new abbot, as has been said before, was supposed to visit the Pope on election, and many travelled in great state, but Richard set out for Avignon (this was at the time of the Great Schism, when there were two rival popes, one in Rome and one at Avignon), in the humblest way, and asked the Abbey exchequer for only thirty shillings for his journey. With his four companions he spent only fifteen pounds altogether, and when he returned there followed a period of rigid economy. He took three years off, to make a leisurely visitation to all the dependent houses up and down the country, and to reform their discipline, relying on the fact that expensive visitors could not very well come to the Abbey while he, their host, was absent.

Being a mathematician he personally audited the accounts of the Abbey and closed up many loopholes in the finances, and with good oversight of administration generally he gradually restored the solvency of the house, and accumulated funds with which to attack the townsfolk and get back the privileges wrung from his predecessor. He opened the campaign by arresting several prominent citizens for moral offences, in his capacity of spiritual ruler of the district. A riot followed in which the Abbey marshal slew one of the prisoners, and was lynched by the infuriated townsmen. The citizens now indicted the Abbot and his servants of murder, hoping that they could pack the jury with their own supporters, since they had the right to exclude "foreigners" from the jury. But this was countered by making up the jury with people from the neighbouring Hundreds, and as these could not be called foreigners, and as the Abbot was quite well liked outside St. Albans, this jury acquitted the defendants. The Abbot now turned the tables by indicting the townspeople, and two royal justices sat at St. Albans to try the case, having been previously feasted by the Abbot, and a number of burgesses were convicted of complicity in the murders and of accusing the Abbot falsely.

The townsmen knew when they were beaten, and had to give in. They gave up their charter of liberties won from Hugh of Eversden, and paid the Abbot forty-eight pounds a year for the use of his fulling mill. They also gave up their own handmills and the Abbot rubbed in his victory by having the stones set in the floor of his parlour as a permanent souvenir. But the result was that the Abbot had spent so much on his campaign that the Abbey was once again short of money, and the Abbot levied a tax on the bondmen of Redbourn. They ingeniously forged a charter to claim that they were exempt, but they had to pay all the same. There were fifty of them, and they were obviously prosperous, for only three of them were excused from payment on the ground of poverty.

Meanwhile, the health of the Abbot gave rise to anxiety, and some of the monks, disaffected on account of the austerity which they suffered, tried to get rid of him by claiming that he had leprosy. Whether this was true or not is unknown. There was some genuine leprosy in England, but most of what was called by that name was more probably some form of eczema. There was, in any case, very little even of that in the neighbourhood. For both the hospitals, St. Julian's and St. Mary de Pratis, which had been founded to house the sufferers from the disease, men and women respectively, had become ordinary cells and had no lepers. There is a manuscript picture of Wallingford, showing him with a face spotted as if he had measles. However, he continued to hold his office until he died in 1335, probably from shock when part of the Abbey was struck by lightning and caught fire. He was a remarkable man, a scientist of distinction, and wrote books on mathematics and astronomy, which he presented to the Abbey library. He invented an astronomical clock, which was still going in the time of Henry VIII, two hundred years later. He was the greatest genius who ever sat in the abbot's stall in St. Albans.

Wallingford was succeeded in 1336 by the second of the great abbots, Michael de Mentmore, who had been the schoolmaster before he entered the Abbey. He was a distinguished scholar, and under his rule the Abbey regained the reputation for culture and good discipline which had been somewhat reduced under Wallingford's predecessors. Mentmore's personal reputation was so great that the Pope gave him the task of holding a series of Chapters to draw up constitutions which should reform the whole Benedictine Order. Having himself been at Oxford, he was interested in sending promising young monks to the university, where the Abbey maintained a separate establishment, Gloucester College. At home, too, studying was made easier by an alteration in the hours of services, so that there might be a longer period for study in the mornings. The library was maintained and added to by a gift of books from the Abbot. But the thirteen years of long and peaceful rule of Mentmore was broken by the tragedy of the Black Death in 1349. The Abbot died of the plague, and with him to the grave went forty-seven monks, over three-quarters of the whole community. The town of St. Albans itself was decimated, and the Death swept like a forest fire through Hertfordshire. It was a dreadful time, and was made worse by a failure of the crops. It would be difficult to estimate the heartbreak and suffering endured at that time by the people who still survived the pestilence, bereavement and starvation.

At this crucial period in the history of St. Albans there came to the Abbey from Tynemouth perhaps the greatest of all the abbots, Thomas de la Mare. He was of aristocratic family, his brother being at one time Speaker of the House of Commons, and he had powerful friends, one of them being the Black Prince, who was on terms of close intimacy with him. He at once set to work reorganising the finances on a more stable basis. For example, instead of the payment of a thousand marks which John of Berkhamsted had promised should be paid on the election of each new abbot, de la Mare arranged that the House should pay fifty marks annually. He also saved money for the future by getting the Pope to dispense with the ceremonial visit to the papal court. He ruled for nearly fifty years, during which he earned the respect and affection of the majority of his monks. The chronicler tells us that he was specially careful about the welfare of the sick, often visiting them and ministering to them with his own hands. He followed Mentmore as President of the General Chapters of the Order, and the king made him his official Visitor of all houses in the king's presentation, with powers of discipline and punishment. In some cases he brought the offenders back with him to St. Albans, where they might learn better ways by the good example set them here. Then he sent them home to teach others how a good monastery should be run. We are not told whether this made him popular with the erring houses, nor whether the presence of their sinful brethren made the St. Albans monks insufferably smug and self-righteous. However, it seemed to work, for other houses actually asked if they could send some of their own monks here to study discipline.

In the political sphere, also, de la Mare was outstanding. Edward III made him a Privy Councillor, and his friendship with the Black Prince led to the presence of a very distinguished visitor at St. Albans in 1356. The Black Prince at the Battle of Poitiers had captured King John of France, and according to custom sent him to England until his ransom had been collected and handed over. The Prince asked his friend de la Mare to look after the king until he could be freed, and he was sent to St. Albans. For some reason, now unknown, he did not go straight to the Abbey, but was housed for a day or two in a private house close to where the Clock Tower was to be built some fifty years later. In years to come this house was to become an inn, named from that royal visit the Fleur-de-Lys. That name is still carried by the public-house which stands on the site, and which itself is very ancient.

But though de la Mare might be well liked in the Abbey and in high places, he was not so popular in the town. Once the chaos caused by the Black Death had cleared up, the townsfolk became prosperous again, and irritation grew ever stronger on lands of all the great monasteries. Vain struggles went on to obtain privileges which had been secured on royal lands centuries earlier, but the abbots still held on to every feudal right, and no monastic town obtained its liberty until the monasteries were swept away in the sixteenth century. Even as late as the mid-fifteenth century, disputes were still going on about the right to have a mill. There is an interesting story from Watford. A certain stranger, John Chertsey, came there to live, and he set up a horsemill and ground barley in defiance of the Abbot's rights. His millstones were seized and carried away in his absence, but his wife waded in, "erupted into execrations and imprecations", and backed up by her friends, whom the chronicler feelingly describes as "of the frail sex, but a rabble of immoderate talkers, lacking in discretion", fought the constables, took back the stones and replaced them in position. The constables appear to have thought discretion the better part of valour in dealing with these ladies and retired, and the Abbot had to take legal action against the husband, who asked pardon on his knees and begged for leave to keep the mill going. But the Abbot was adamant, and Chertsey finally gave in and pulled down the mill. One wonders what his gallant wife said to her pusillanimous husband. Somehow one does not picture *her* on her knees to the Abbot.

When the so-called Peasants' Revolt broke out in 1381, it was not the St. Albans serfs who were the leaders, for they had mostly gained nearly all their personal freedom as time had gone by, and serfdom was almost ended. But it was the well-to-do burghers, the middle classes, who were in the forefront of the struggle against the Abbey. While there were some outbreaks of violence in other parts of the country, the rebels showed considerable restraint and discipline in St. Albans. Some of them went to London to join Wat Tyler, the leader—and the Prior and some of the monks went to Tynemouth, about as far as they could get from the point of danger! The Abbot, however, and the majority of the monks stayed at their posts, though perhaps they had qualms when some of the local lads started pulling down the fences round the Abbot's warren of Shropshirelane (round about where the City Station is now), and setting prisoners free from the Abbey gaol.

The Abbot found it best to bow to the storm and grant to the citizens the right to have their own court. Deputations began to arrive from Watford, Rickmansworth, Berkhamsted, and other places on the Abbey lands, each seeking a grant of special demands. The men of Redbourn wanted to hunt rabbits in the Abbot's special warren and to fish in the Ver, the men of Barnet wanted the right to sell their land if they wished. Some of the rioters, becoming more violent, broke into the Abbey by way of the Great Gateway. This had only recently been rebuilt, after an older one had been destroyed in a great storm which lasted five days, and blew down the spire of Norwich Cathedral. The Abbot deemed it prudent to grant a charter of liberties, very much like that which had been forced from Hugh of Eversden, except that the clause demanding to choose their own members of Parliament was omitted when the Abbot explained that if he did not choose the representatives he would not pay their expenses. As membership of Parliament in those days was not at all popular the townsfolk dropped that demand.

De la Mare endeavoured to come to terms with the rebels, and tried to buy off the leader, William Grindcobbe, by offering him his life if he would induce the rebels to disperse. The monk who reports this called Grindcobbe a "son of Belial", but his obvious hatred cannot disguise the nobility of this early St. Albans hero. "Friends," he said, "who after so long an age of oppression have at last won for yourselves a short breath of freedom, hold firm while you can, and have no thought of me or what I may suffer. For if I die for the cause of the liberty we have won, I shall think myself happy to end my life as a martyr. Act now as you would have acted supposing that I had been beheaded at Hertford yesterday." The St. Albans monk who tells the story gloats over the brutal penalty this hero paid for the fight for freedom, but his modern fellow-citizens can be grateful to him for reporting those noble words.

When the revolt collapsed, young King Richard II came to the town with a large number of armed men. A number of prisoners were brought from Hertford for trial, including the famous preacher, John Ball, perhaps the first English Socialist. The court was held in the Moot Hall, before Judge Tressilian. The jurors refused to indict Grindcobbe and two others, named Cadynton and Barber, and had to be harangued by the judge, who finally, by a stratagem, obtained an indictment by some of the jurors. These three defendants were executed and others were imprisoned. The townspeople turned round and accused the Abbot of being the cause of the trouble, and only withdrew the accusation under threats of heavy penalties. Some citizens took down the bodies of the executed, which were hanging in chains just outside the town boundary, as was customary, and it was only by threats that they were induced to replace them on the gibbets. For this exploit they were fined, and the fines had to be paid to the Abbot at the next Saturday market. The trouble did not die down, however, but was followed by outbreaks of incendiarism at Sandridge, Walden and Codicote. The townsfolk continued their efforts to get down the bodies, changing their plea to the grounds of health. They were finally allowed to have their way by the request of Anne of Bohemia, Richard's gentle queen. Of course the charters were annulled, and henceforth the relations between town and Abbey grew ever more bitter. The fact that the villeins had mainly gained their personal freedom was due to economic causes and did not benefit the burgesses. But even the serfs were finally freed only slowly as is shown by some entries, as late as 1466, getting on for a hundred years after the rising. Two serfs from Sandridge, William and Robert Nasshe, and two from Baldock, Thomas at Wode and his brother John, were freed in that year. But as far as we know the burgesses made no further attempts to win their right to govern themselves.

The great historical writer of the Abbey at this time was Thomas Walsingham. His work is remarkable for the bitter attacks he made on the government of his day, and he especially hated John of Gaunt, probably for his protection of John Wyclif. One of these attacks was so bitter that it was suppressed, and exists only in fragments. Another of his works was a continuation of Paris's Lives of the Abbots and his chronicle is the most important source of English history for his time. He was not the only historical writer at the Abbey at the time. Several turned out works of great importance, with the result that the library began to outgrow its accommodation, and de la Mare was about to build a new library when he died in 1396.

Once more the finances of the House were in a very precarious state. Hospitality had become an insupportable burden. People were becoming more materialistic, and pilgrimages no longer formed a paying source of income. Religious houses all over the country were becoming very unpopular. Great people no longer came with rich gifts, but used the Abbey as a country hotel without the necessity of paying their way. They often put a heavy burden on the funds of the House, and went away frequently without leaving anything much by way of recompense. They sometimes brought an army of retainers. Humphrey, Duke of Gloucester, who is buried in the Abbey, whose wife was a member of the Fraternity and who counted himself a friend of a later Abbot, once brought three hundred men with him and expected the Abbey to provide board and lodging for them for a fortnight. Truly an odd way of showing friendship! In 1459, Henry VI spent Easter at the Abbey, and before leaving ordered his best robe to be given to the Abbey, but the royal treasurer got together with the Prior and redeemed it for fifty marks, as it was needed. He probably made a hard bargain, for fifty marks would hardly compensate for the entertainment of the king and his entourage over Easter, and the transaction throws a lurid light on the royal finances, if it is true that the king (suffering from mental trouble, be it noted), could not spare his best robe, "as it was needed". The daughter Houses could not help for they were themselves in debt. Tynemouth was damaged by Scottish forays, and the Abbot had to ask the king for help towards the repair of that House. The revenues from the estates were not enough to pay the running expenses, and as the fifteenth century went on the Abbey finances became more and more involved, so that the House was constantly verging on bankruptcy.

The next abbot, John Moote, had a short reign of only five years, but during that time he managed to strain the finances still further by building a fine country house at Tyttenhanger as an official country holiday home for the abbots. It was reputed to be the finest monastic country residence in the realm. But Moote's successor, John Heyworth, was a young man, and so far from using Tyttenhanger and taking his ease, he left St. Albans for a time to live in strict economy while he visited the dependent Houses. He evidently had some private means, for he asked nothing from the cells of the House in the way of money for his expenses. As a result the finances began to recover. Some years later he left St. Albans to become Bishop of Lichfield. During his rule, the Abbey had been seriously worried by the town becoming a hotbed of Lollardy. The Lollards were early reformers, who followed the doctrine of John Wyclif, and the Church recognised them as dangerous to religious authoritarianism. Showers of Lollard leaflets appeared mysteriously in the streets, and the leader of the Lollards, Sir John Oldcastle, hid near St. Albans for a while and had plenty of friends in the town.

At this time St. Albans saw one of its surviving landmarks arise—the Clock Tower. This was built between 1402 and 1411, and is the only example of a town belfry in this country, except that of Morpeth in Northumberland, which, however, also performed the duty of a watchtower against border raids. The bell which was hung there to ring the curfew was older than the tower, being cast in 1335, and it bears the inscription, "Missi de coelis habeo nomen Gabrielis". (I bear heaven-sent Gabriel's name.) It may be that the Abbey acquired some new bells about this time, and that the Abbot presented

The Abbey, from across the Lake

Verulamium : a model of the London Gate

Verulamium : The Scallopshell Mosaic

Verulamium

(left) Bronze Statue of Venus

(below) The Lion Pavement

The Great Gateway of the Abbey

St. Albans Abbey : A Reconstruction by Charles W. Ashdown

The Antelope Inn, originally the Great Guesthouse of the Abbey

Fishpool Street

St. Michael's Street

Sir Nicholas Bacon's Gorhambury

Holywell House, the Home of the Duchess of Marlborough

An Election in the Early Nineteenth Century: The Hustings in
front of the Clock Tower

The Abbey before Restoration, from an etching by Capt. James Gape, 1822

"View from the New Turnpike, the improved road, etc., St. Albans, *c.* 1758"

The Abbey after Restoration (*etching by F. G. Kitton*)

The Pedestal of the Shrine of St. Alban
in the Saint's Chapel, St. Albans Abbey,
after restoration

Queen Elizabeth the Queen Mother, receiving the Freedom of the City, April 13th. 1961

The Market

The Marlborough Almshouses

one of the old ones to the town, but that is merely conjecture.

Heyworth was followed by John of Wheathampstead, a local man, whose mother owned property at Mackerye End. He was a famous scholar, and the Abbey saw brilliant gatherings of well-known people, among whom were Humphrey Duke of Gloucester (brother of Henry V), whose body is buried in the Abbey in the Saint's Chapel. The vault is covered by a trap-door, and when it is opened some steps lead down to a grated door through which one can see the corner of the coffin.

The indiscipline of the monks was a sore trial to Wheathampstead. He attended the Council of Pavia, but before he went he issued a set of regulations which tell the tale of an unsatisfactory atmosphere—nothing seriously wrong, but a don't care attitude to their religious reputation. They were instructed not to stand about talking to women, not to be seen drinking when they were supposed to be in service, and not to indulge in horseplay. Alas for the traditions of the past! John de Cella must have been turning in his grave. The monks yearned for the fleshpots of this world, and got some of them (including better suppers), according to the chronicler. The scriptorium declined. Wheathampstead saw all this happening, and he spent his time fighting for improvement, but the feeling of the House was against him, and he was not the man to be a despot, perhaps unfortunately, for it might have been better for the Abbey to have felt the hand of a master.

He was also engaged in a continual struggle with the tenants of the Abbey, not the burgesses, but the knights and noblemen and lawyers, who paid rents for their lands in the modern fashion, or, at least, were supposed to pay rents. The unfortunate Abbot was involved over and over again in lawsuits to maintain the rights of the House, in some cases winning by bribery, in others by expedients which came precious near fraud. For example, he had to join battle with the Bishop of Norwich, who claimed a tax which John said was not due, as Offa had exempted the House from any jurisdiction by outsiders in St. Albans. Of course, Offa had done nothing of the sort, as is plain from the copy of his charter in the Cottonian MS, but the Abbot put forward a

version which had a number of additions inserted—an outrageous forgery. We cannot prove that Wheathampstead
was the forger, but the bishop had to give him best. In 1440
the matter was settled by an elaborate confirmation of the
charter of Henry II, which had the effect of making the
Abbot a petty king in his domain.

The king handed over all his rights in the matter of justice,
giving the Abbot jurisdiction over all men within the lands
of the Abbey, that he should have all fines, all treasure trove,
and hold all courts in the Liberty of St. Albans, and he could
appoint his own justices to keep peace, and the justices of the
peace for the county were not to interfere. Even when the
king's judges were holding court within the Liberty, the
bailiff of the Abbot and the Abbot's coroner (a strange term,
since the coroner is the crowner, i.e. a king's officer), were to
be there to call the juries and carry out the judgments of the
royal judges. The Abbot should have the assize of bread,
wine, ale, meat and drink, weights and measures, fixing prices
and standards, and taking all fines from offences regarding
them, with no interference from the clerk of the market of the
king's household. Nor was the king to requisition from the
Abbot or any of his tenants' horses, carts, animals or corn
without permission of the Abbot. It may well be that the
section whereby the county magistrates were forbidden to
administer justice within the Liberty is the origin of the
separate commission of the peace which St. Albans still
enjoys. Until 1948 the city still had its own police force,
which was, after that date, merged with the county force,
but the separation of the courts remained for some years.

Despite the unsatisfactory atmosphere in the Abbey, there
yet were faithful souls who put in their best work to the glory
of God. In the *Annales* of John de Amundesham we are told,
about 1430, "Opposite the altar of St. Sith, lies Brother
William Stubbarde, formerly lay brother of this house, a
praiseworthy worker in masonry, whose good works shown in
the cloister, the Prior's seat there, and the doors and other
laudable works at Redbourn and Beaulieu, have as we believe,
ensured the passage of his soul to Heaven".

The accumulated worries of Wheathamstead had the
result of giving him a nervous breakdown, and he resigned in

1440, just after receiving the Charter, and he was succeeded by John Stoke, Prior of Wallingford. The previous abbot was pensioned, and we do not know whether he remained in the Abbey or retired to his country house, Mackerye End, which he had inherited from his mother. Probably he did the latter, as he quarrelled with Stoke. When the Pope gave Wheathampstead some benefices, Stoke tried to stop his pension, and when his rather mean trick was defeated, gave vent to his spite and did what he could to injure his predecessor. Stoke seems to have been a quarrelsome individual, for he fell out with other dignitaries of the Abbey and with its cells, one of which, Wymondham, refused any longer to acknowledge the authority of St. Albans, and became an independent monastery. At home, several monks just walked out, and some obtained the Pope's permission to join the rebellious house of Wymondham. Stoke became the most-hated man in the Abbey, and this shows clearly in the account written by the author of the register of John of Wheathampstead, our chief authority for the history of the Abbey at this period. When Stoke died in 1451 the candidates who were invited all refused to stand for election; the monks wanted Wheathampstead back, and though now an ageing man, he was persuaded, and resumed his Abbacy to the joy of all the monks. It is interesting to read that after his return several of the monks who had gone to Wymondham came to St. Albans and pleaded to be taken back, and some were re-admitted.

Wheathampstead added to the landed property of the Abbey by purchasing the manors of Garston near Watford, and Agnells in Redbourn, and land within the manor of Squyllers, which took in the middle of St. Albans and had partly fallen into private hands, and he also bought the manor of Moor, which is possibly Moor Park. If so, the geography of his biographer went wrong somewhat, for he says that by the purchase the Abbot acquired a beautiful house and a fine position on the banks of the Thames in the City of London!

CHAPTER SEVEN

THE LAST YEARS OF THE MONASTERY

IT was well that there was a wise man at the head of affairs at this troublous time, for the Wars of the Roses were to break out within four years, and twice St. Albans saw the armies fight in its streets. The Abbey was probably divided in its opinions, but the Abbot managed to keep more or less neutral, though this very neutrality put the House in danger, for both sides threatened to sack it, and the Lancastrians did.

The first battle took place in 1455. The king, Henry VI, with his wife, Margaret of Anjou, were staying in St. Albans, not at the Abbey, but in the home of one Edmond Westby, who lived at a house called Hall Place, in the Bowgate. The Yorkist army lay to the east of the town, and probably the Earl of Warwick was staying with his brother, the Earl of Salisbury, at the nearby Salisbury Hall, near London Colney. On the morning of the battle the king held a council in the Moot Hall. His forces numbered over two thousand men, according to the record in *Archaeologia*. His banner was pitched in St. Peter's Street, and a strong watch was set at the various bars. The Yorkists mustered in Keyfield, the field outside the boundary, the name being now attached to a car-park. The Duke of York sent a conciliatory message to the king, but the reply hotly rejected it and threatened hanging, drawing and quartering to all who were guilty of fighting against their king. As the king was suffering from mental trouble, and probably did not fully realise what was going on, one can detect the voice of the fiery Margaret in this message. The Yorkist army then broke through the defences behind the present Chequer Street, between the Cross Keys Inn (which vanished when the present London Road was cut through to the High Street in the early nineteenth century). and the Chequers Inn, now, reduced in size, the Queen's Head. A discovery in 1958 of the remains of a fifteenth-century private house, which must have been next door to the Keys, shows that the house was set sideways to the road, and probably had a garden at the side, which would have offered no obstacle to the passage of the army once it was over the Tonman Ditch, by this time the chief part of the town's defences. With a shout of "A Warwick! A Warwick!" the army surged into Chequer Street and thence to St. Peter's Street, where they joined battle with the Lancastrians. One of the leading nobles, the Duke of Somerset, died on the steps of the Castle Inn, which stood where a bank now stands on the corner of Victoria Street. The king, wounded in the neck, took refuge in a poor man's house—tradition says a tanner—and was captured and taken to the Abbey and thence, next day, to London, as a prisoner in all but name.

The second battle was six years later. This time the Yorkists occupied the town and the Lancastrians, led by Queen Margaret, came from the north by Watling Street. She advanced up George Street, then called Church Lane, but found that there was a strong barricade there, too strong for her to break through. Years ago, when new drains were being laid outside a shop now occupied by a large draper, a rusty crossbow was found by the workmen. It has survived in private hands but not in St. Albans. It was obviously a relic of that battle. Margaret then retreated down George Street and Fishpool Street, and got across to Folly Lane and along the line of the Tonman Ditch to the Catherine Bar, which, surprisingly, was only lightly defended, and she broke through, cutting the Yorkist army in half. The greater part retreated to Bernard's Heath, where they were completely defeated, the remnants fleeing to Nomansland to their death there. The Earl of Warwick lost the king in the turmoil, and he was found sitting under an oak tree laughing gently at what was going on. He was clearly still out of his mind, though harmless. His queen came up and met her husband possibly for the first time for six years; she celebrated her victory by handing over the town to her soldiery with leave to loot at their pleasure. There ensued perhaps the worst night in the history of St. Albans, when hundreds of soldiers ravaged the town, looting and killing. She herself was not backward in this respect, and when she went the Abbey's best jewel went with her.

There is conflicting opinion as to the state of the Abbey at this time. It was a period when all sorts of charges of immorality and bad discipline were hurled at the religious houses, irrespective of whether there was any ground for them, and modern historians have ranged themselves on different sides. Henry Froude believed anything he read against the monasteries, while Abbé Gasquet was equally prejudiced in their favour. It is difficult at this time to tell what was actually the truth. The Abbey was to face enemies in the new régime when the Tudors came to the throne, for while it had successfully sat on the fence for quite a while during the dynastic wars, it had eventually come down on the side of the Yorkists, and this did not endear it to Cardinal Morton, Henry VII's Archbishop of Canterbury and Chancellor of England, who wanted to get over the Abbey's exemption from visitation. Though the Pope warned him that he had no authority, he tried to bluff, and sent an "admonition" to Abbot Wallingford, accusing him of all sorts of scandals, which were in all probability lies, and at worst highly exaggerated, since St. Albans was so near London that matters could not have been as bad as suggested without a public scandal long before, and there is no evidence from other sources that there was anything of the sort.

The Pope allowed just one visitation in 1490. There is no record of the result; in fact, there is no evidence that it ever took place, but if it did then the Archbishop must have realised that he had no case, for there was no publicity, and the Abbot was not driven to resign, as would inevitably have happened had the charges been proved. He continued to rule over the Abbey, and the only conclusion is that rumour lied. Froude, of course, believed the worst, but modern opinion feels that things could not have been too bad, though one must admit, on the other hand, that the state of the Abbey was far from perfect.

It is to Wallingford that we owe the lovely high altar screen, which took about twenty years a-building. During this time, printing came to England, and in time superseded the old method of making books by hand-copying, and thereby did away with one of the last excuses for the existence of the great monasteries. Now others took over the work of producing books, and these others were laymen. The first printing press was set up within the precincts of Westminster Abbey, but St. Albans was not far behind. About 1482 a press was set up by a man whose name we do not know. All we can say is that he was called the "Schoolmaster-Printer of St. Albans". From the fact that one of the books he printed began with the words "Insomuch as", he has been nicknamed John Insomuch. In all, he produced eight books before his press ceased in 1488. Where the press was we do not know; it is unlikely to have been in the Abbey itself, since the schoolmaster was not a monk, but it may have been set up on the school premises. He produced a *Chronicle of England* and the famous *Book of St. Albans*. A legend grew up that this was the work of a prioress of Sopwell named Juliana Berners or Barnes, but there can be no truth in this, as there never was a prioress of that name, nor was there a contemporary Berners lady named Juliana. So very regretfully we have to give up our claim to the very first woman writer on sports, especially as the chapter on fishing is said to be the best before *The Compleat Angler*. Although our anonymous schoolmaster ceased to function as a printer in 1488, his press was revived fifty years later by John Hertford, who printed a life of St. Alban and St. Amphibalus. Hertford later moved from St. Albans, and set up his equipment in Aldersgate, where it was used for a time by a Nicholas Boreman. This name is intriguing. Could he have been a kinsman of Richard Boreman, the last Abbot? The chief output of the St. Albans press consisted of scholarly works, whereas Caxton catered for the general reader—already the distinction between fiction and non-fiction held the germ of our modern library classification.

Wallingford died in 1492, and with him died the last remnants of the greatness of the Abbey. The mediaeval period was over, and in the world of the Tudors the monastery was an anachronism. Ramryge, probably a member of a local family, since the name occurs often in the neighbourhood, succeeded him. His beautiful little chantry tomb in the Abbey bears the rebus on his name—a ram prancing on a ridge. He did his rather poor best to prevent the Abbey sinking into decline and bankruptcy, but so powerless did he become that he found himself unable to get rid of incompetent officials—he tried in vain to sack the keeper of the gaol and the Abbey porter, and the master of St. Julian's Hospital. The Prioress of Sopwell ceased to be a submissive subordinate, and accused him of altering a lease to the disadvantage of her house. The Abbot of Westminster at last asserted his right to be premier abbot and won the centuries-old battle.

Unfortunately the returns of Hertfordshire to Henry VIII's *Valor Ecclesiasticus*, which gives the details of monastic finances, are missing. They could give us precious information, but there is only a compressed summary extant, and that tells us little, except that we can read between the lines and see a shaking off of the yoke of the Abbey by townsfolk and customary tenants alike. Offices such as the clerk of the markets and the bailiff were farmed out to townspeople for payment of a lump sum.

The Abbey was no longer departmentalised. The monks all received an allowance from which they paid for their board and lodging. Most of the revenue went on running expenses, with numbers of servants and officials to be paid salaries. At the same time there was a steady rise in prices, owing to changes in the economy of the country generally, yet the burden of hospitality remained. Some pilgrims still came, and Wallingford had allowed one of the local innkeepers to fit up a chapel for the use of guests crowded out of the Abbey guesthouse, and there is reason to believe that this was not a solitary instance.

There is an interesting description of life in the Abbey just before the Dissolution, found quoted in a description of St. Albans in 1814. The statement is said to be taken from *The Antiquarium Repertory*, vol. 3, p. 60, and is quoted as from "a loose paper in Mr. Ashmole's handwriting, 26th August, 1688, in the library of the late Thos. Astle, esquire".

"Mr. Robert Shrimpton, grandfather by the mother's side to Mrs. Simpson of St. Albans, was four times mayor of that town. He died about sixty years ago, being then about 103 years of age. He lived when the Abbey of St. Albans flourished, before the Dissolution and remembered most things relating to the buildings of the Abbey, the Regimen of the House, the Ceremonies of the Church and grand processions; of all of which he would often discourse in his lifetime. Among other things, that in the Great Hall, there was an ascent of fifteen steps to the Abbot's table, to which the Monks brought up the service in plate and staying at every fifth step, which was a landing-place, on every of which they sung a short Hymn. The Abbot usually sat alone in the middle of the table, and when any Nobleman or Embassador or Stranger of eminent quality came hither, they sat at his table towards the ends thereof. After the Monks had waited awhile on the Abbot, they sat down at two other tables placed on the sides of the Hall and had their Services brought in by the Novices who, when the Monks had dined, sat down to their own dinner. This Mr. Shrimpton remembered that when the news came of Queen Mary's death, the Abbot for grief took to his chamber and dyed in a fortnight." (This relates to the period after the Dissolution, when there had been a suggestion under Mary that the monastery should be reinstated.)

"He also remembered the hollow image erected near St. Alban's shrine wherein, One being placed to govern the wires, the Eyes would move and Head nod according as he liked or disliked the offering, and being young he had many times crept into the hollow part thereof. In the grand procession through the town where the Image of St. Alban was carried, it was usually borne by two Monks, and after it had been set down awhile at the Market Cross, and the Monks assaying to take it away, they pretended they could not stir it, then the Abbot coming and laying his Crosier upon the Image, and saying these words, 'Arise, arise, St. Alban, and get thee home to thy Sanctuary', it then forthwith yielded to be borne by the Monks. In the Abbey there was a large room having beds set on either side for the receipt of Strangers and Pilgrims, where they had Lodging and Diet for three days without Question made whence they came or whither they went; but after that they stayed not without rendering an account of both."

It would seem from this vivid account that the Abbot and his guests could never have had a really hot meal. One can imagine the unfortunate diners, hungry perhaps after their journey, waiting impatiently while the monks sang those three hymns on their way up to the high table. Let us hope that they were very short ones.

The details seem just what a garrulous old man would remember of his youth. The mumbo-jumbo of the nodding image and its obstinacy by the Eleanor Cross does not seem to have deceived the sharp-eyed youngster, and probably caused some sarcastic remarks among the onlookers. Robert Shrimpton, by the way, was mayor for the first time in 1588, again in 1595, and a third time in 1605, but there appears to be no record of the fourth term mentioned.

Ramryge died in 1519, and to the dismay of the monks the abbacy was given to Cardinal Wolsey. It was a flagrant insult to the Abbey, for never before had it been so despised that it was not considered necessary for there to be a resident Abbot, who was Abbot and nothing else. Probably Wolsey knew its hopeless condition, and he wanted to get some of the loot for his proposed foundations at Oxford and Ipswich. He suppressed the cells at Wallingford and St. Mary de Pré, though suppressing the latter was rather like shutting the stable door when the horse was gone, for on the death of the Prioress the nuns, reduced to five in number, had recently decided to close down and just walked out, leaving the place empty. Wolsey alienated any property of value belonging to these foundations. He never resided at St. Albans, but one must be just and admit that he asserted the ancient liberties of the House and defended it from the exactions of royal officials.

On the disgrace and death of Wolsey in 1530 the abbacy passed to Prior Robert Catton, who had run the Abbey as Wolsey's deputy. He was obsequious and subservient to Thomas Cromwell, and he diddled the Abbey out of the property of Childwick for the benefit of Cromwell's friend, Cavendish, Wolsey's faithful secretary, who wrote his biography. Catton lined the pockets of his friends at the expense of the Abbey. The monks appealed to an enemy of Cromwell, and therefore of the Abbot, but without success. In 1536 many of the cells suffered dissolution along with the smaller monasteries. In the autumn of 1537 the royal Visitors came to St. Albans, and it was reported that they found ample reasons for sacking the Abbot. In 1538 he was deposed, though Cromwell arranged a pension of eighty pounds a year for him, chargeable on the Abbey, which, it is pleasant to record was never paid. Later a gossip wrote, "St. Albans is not yet suppressed, but it is daily looked for".

Richard Boreman was appointed Abbot and was destined to be the last of a long line. He did his utmost to stave off the inevitable. He found the finances so bad that he was actually sent to prison for failing to pay dues to the king. He held on and managed to pay what was due at the end of 1538, but in December 1539 the impossible financial situation compelled him to surrender the House into the king's hands, a thing he had said he would never do. Some modern writers have stated that he was put into the position merely because he was pliable and would surrender without hesitation, but this can hardly be the case, in view of his year and a half's struggle to keep going. The facts speak for themselves.

There were thirty-eight monks in the Abbey at the end. They received small pensions, but since they were normally of the aristocratic upper class, as has already been said, this was probably not too great a hardship. The Abbot received a pension of £226 13s. 4d. This was a very large pension, the equivalent of at least eight thousand pounds in 1975. One can compare it with the "golden handshake" in modern take-over bids between commercial firms. The people to feel inconvenience were the distinguished people who had looked on the Abbey as a place of entertainment on the cheap. And the School disappeared, fortunately only temporarily. It was not a charitable institution, but one of social standing. Only the sixteen poorest scholars paid no fees. In the fourteenth century had begun the custom of receiving a few poor boys entitled to receive free education in the School, which thus grew a little more democratic in tone. The master was no longer a cleric, but a layman, as we know from the fact that one of them, in his will, leaves his goods to his wife. He had the sole right of secular education in St. Albans, which was the centre for the whole neighbourhood. By a stretch of legal terms it was considered a part of the Abbey property, and by its closure a blow was aimed at local education which must have caused much anxiety in the district.

Twelve days after the surrender, officials loaded up vehicles with the sacred vessels and the treasures of the shrine, which were taken away for the king's use. It was estimated that there were over a hundred ounces of pure gold and over four thousand ounces of silver-gilt. This was, of course, only the weight, and the value of the melted metals took no account of the value as works of art. Next, workmen started pulling down the conventual buildings of the Abbey. One wonders what were the thoughts of the onlookers as they saw the familiar buildings vanish, but there is no record of any protest being made. In the end, all was pulled down except the church, the Great Gateway, and the long line of stables. These last remained in use until the eighteenth century, and it is probable that the destruction of the other buildings took many years to accomplish, for the amount of building material must have taken time to dispose of, and would not have fetched much if there were a glut at any one time. No doubt much of it went on building in St. Albans and the neighbourhood, and there must have been a number of shops and houses new or rebuilt with cheap stone and timber.

The monastic buildings with all the land surrounding them were granted to Sir Richard Lee, a military engineer, and a friend of Henry VIII, but he sold the site to Boreman and his heirs in the fifth year of Edward VI. The price paid was £586 13s 4d. In terms of present-day prices this would be at least £10,000, and it is clear that Boreman must have been a wealthy man. The following year, when the town got its first charter, the citizens acquired the Abbey church from the king for £400, a good example of the town's municipal enterprise.

Boreman had been deeply affected by the closure of the School, and he made plans for its revival. The religious guilds had been suppressed under Edward VI; one of these in St. Albans was the Brotherhood of the Charnel House, which had a hall on the corner of St. Peter's churchyard. The guild had owned a good deal of property in the town, including the Bear Inn, the Well House on Holywell Hill, the Bull Inn, a house called Lymberies, also on Holywell Hill, the Crane in

Fishpool Street, the Brotherhood House which seems to have been in the Market Place, and had been used as a moot hall by the burgesses in the days of the monastery, land in Bowgate in St. Peter's Street, land on Bernard's Heath and in London Colney and Eywood. Now Boreman thought the St. Peter's churchyard property would make good premises for a school. He obtained a private Act of Parliament permitting him to set up a free school in the town, and in the Chantry Certificates of 1538 in the Public Record Office there is a note against the entry of the Charnel House, "Richard Bawrman, late Abbote of Seynt Albons sueth to purchase this and to erect a scole there". Whether he ever set up his school is unknown, but it may have been so, and when the town became a municipality in 1553 he handed over his permission to the corporation, and the School was housed in the Lady Chapel, which became detached from the main building by the erection of a wall. Another wall running parallel to this behind the Saint's Chapel gave a public footpath through from north to south, which remained in use until the restoration of the abbey by Lord Grimthorpe in the late nineteenth century. This use of the Lady Chapel was a sensible one, for the town had no particular use for the parts of the church which had been reserved to the monastic community and not normally open to the public; to have left them unoccupied would have probably meant their becoming ruinous. At the same time they had to find a home for the School, and to house the School in the Lady Chapel provided a solution to two problems.

And so passed one of the most important institutions in the country, and there is no record of anyone grieving bitterly thereat except Boreman. During the reign of Mary Tudor there was a suggestion that the Abbey should be revived, and Boreman made a deed of gift of all the Abbey property he owned to the queen, but the proposal came to nothing. Mary died, and so did the Abbot, of grief it is said. Some of his family lived on in St. Albans, and a clergyman named George Boreman was Vicar of St. Peter's a few years later, while another of the name was Vicar of Redbourn.

CHAPTER EIGHT

LIFE IN MEDIAEVAL ST. ALBANS

THE dissolution of the Monastery marked virtually the end of the mediaeval period at St. Albans, and one may profitably pause here to consider something of the daily life of the town as it had existed.

The main streets were those of the centre of the city today, and their names are quite recognisable despite mediaeval spelling. Halywelstrete included both Holywell Hill and Chequer Street, and led down to Halywellbrygge. The modern George Street was then known as Chyrchstrete or Lane, and occasionally we find it called Cook Lane. It is curious that it was not called George Street until probably the late seventeenth century, although the George Inn was in existence very early, taking its name from the saint, not as is sometimes mistakenly thought, from one of the Hanoverian kings. It is sometimes found with the name of the George upon the Hupe or Hoop, and may have had a hoop hanging as part of its sign. Fysshepolestrete is quite recognisable, despite the passion of our ancestors never to use one letter where ten would do. Skolelane is somewhat puzzling, since there was only one School, and that was not in a lane; once the School had been transferred to the Lady Chapel in the 1550's, the Waxhousegate Lane was called School Lane, but that was over a hundred years later than the other Skolelane, whose position we do not know. Some of the outskirts are named. Parke Stret and Barnet Hethe lie on the south and the north of the town respectively. The transition from Barnet Heath to the modern Bernard's Heath is interesting and difficult to explain. A meadow "lying near the end of the town" is called Grenesmede, which can be identified as the site of the estate of council houses known as New Green's. The present High Street was generally known in the middle ages as the Vintry, as the Abbey vineyard occupied the land now belonging to a bank, and running down to the Sumpter Yard, though as a matter of fact the Vintry and George

Street were called the Heigh Strete in the survey of St. Albans carried out in the reign of Mary Tudor.

Many of the aspects of daily life can be seen in the carvings on the watching loft in the Abbey. They show how rural the life still was. Here is a man reaping wheat with a sickle, while another carries a sheaf for stooking, and in another bit of carving a man and woman are sitting with a basket between them containing loaves. Another shows a hunter with his bow, blowing his horn, while his dog sits by him. There is a very smart lady sitting, perhaps waiting for her lover, her hands folded on her lap. A shepherd plays a double recorder, and one of his sheep scratches its ear with one foot. Two men wrestle and a woman sits spinning while a cow and calf graze nearby. There is a sow and her litter, a hart, the badge of Richard II and of the county. A cow is being milked, though one does not envy the milkmaid her very uncomfortable position, a bear is being chained up and another bear, muzzled, is ready for the attack by three dogs.

There were many religious feasts, all of which were observed as holidays; shops were shut and the craftsmen went in procession through the streets carrying guild banners, and possibly performing scenes on carts which moved from stand to stand in the town. In Bales' *Chronicle* there is an entry of 1443: "Item this yer was at seint albons the last of Juyn a play of Eglemour and Degrebelle." This is a unique entry. There is no record of the playing of these romances in any other chronicle. Usually they were "mystery" plays, as at York. Mystery means craft and these were attached to particular crafts. Market day was held every week, and there are references to people being punished for selling in the market without permission. After 1553 all stallholders had to be freemen, and there must have been some similar restriction earlier. The market was divided into zones. The malt market was in the lower part of Chequer Street, and the hay market near the present town hall at the top of the same street. The shambles, fleshshambles or meat market, was in the lower part of the Market Place, and the fish market on the Dagnall Street side of the present town hall. The women's market, or butter market, where the women sold butter, cheese, eggs and chickens, was in French Row, which was sometimes called Cordwainers' Row, where the shoemakers had their shops. The wheat cheaping and the leather shambles lay in the market between French Row and Dagnall Street, and the nuns of the Pré had a walled garden and one or two houses in French Row. There was also a part of the market called the pudding shamble, and the passage behind the modern corn exchange is Pudding Lane.

The north side of Romeland was known as Hokerhulle and the lower part of Fishpool Street was, and is still, though few know it, the Sallypath, perhaps connected with the entrance to Kingsbury Castle, in which case it must be the oldest street name in the city, dating from Saxon times. In the Sallypath there was an ancient house, mentioned in 1388 and in ruins in Tudor times, called Coppedhall, which belonged to St. Bartholomew's Priory, Smithfield. The district round St. Michael's Bridge was Gonnerston or Gunnerstone, the stone perhaps being the lump outside Kingsbury Mill. A road ran partly along the line of Branch Road, but deviated across the field to the north, where a ridge can still be seen running over to the entrance to Batchwood Drive. This latter, until the council house estate was laid out, was still a winding lane leading to the lane now Waverley Road and to Harpenden Road. Another road branched from Gunnerstone, rather to the south of Branch Road, and the line is now covered up by buildings, but it joined Folly Lane, then called Claypits Lane. There was a cross, St. John's Cross, here. There was another cross, the Black Cross or Stone Cross, at the beginning of Sandpit Lane, and still another, the Red Cross, at the junction of London Road and the lane leading to Cell Barnes.

All the innyards of Holywell Hill and Chequer Street on the east side ran down to the Monk Ditch, which seems to have run parallel to the Tonman Ditch on the town side, with a path running its length called the Houndspath. Grange Street was then St. Peter's Lane and a house, the Lamb, stood near the corner of Catherine Street. There are numerous documents in the city archives relating to this property, which belonged to St. Peter's Church, and had land alongside. It seems to have stretched partly down Catherine Street and along St. Peter's Street the other way. In 1962 an old public house, the Queen Adelaide was remodelled. The architect found it to be, behind a Victorian front, a building at least five hundred years old, and it is possible that it was originally a part of the house, the Lamb, which was probably but not necessarily an inn.

There was a parish pound at the corner of St. Peter's Road, and a duck pond at St. Peter's Green. Altogether there were three ponds in St. Peter's Street, one where the present Market Square is. Dagnall Street was sometimes called Bothel Street, and it continued to the Watling Street via Wellclose Street.

Three times a year there was a fair, usually held on Romeland. Here would come merchants and pedlars to do business, and jugglers, acrobats, musicians and dancers to amuse the citizens. Because so many of these people were strangers who would be here today and gone tomorrow, there was a Court of Pie Powder, the court which dealt out summary jurisdiction, and sat continuously until the fair was over. It was very necessary, for the "foreigners" from other parts of the country, and some even foreigners in our sense of the word, were not noted for their honesty, and many a St. Albans housewife would have found herself cheated of the proper length of a roll of cloth, or fobbed off with an inferior weave, unless she could immediately complain to the official of the Abbot who presided over the "Court of the Dusty Feet".

The inhabitants of the town were of many types and occupations. Many were traders, craftsmen who made the wares they sold in the rooms behind their shops, some probably sold goods from outside and were middlemen; there were lawyers (some of them in the pay of the Abbey), doctors and barber-surgeons and scriveners, who usually specialised in conveyancing.

Of sports, hunting was reserved for the Abbot and his friends; a few of the more important burgesses may have had permission to own hawks. On the north of St. Albans is a hospital known by the name of Oster Hills. The word Oster means probably that hawking went on there, or perhaps that hawks were kept there, though the *Gesta* says Oster Hills was so called because of the quantity of oyster shells found. Of course, the Romans ate quantities of oysters, but it is a little much to believe that they came at least a mile outside the city to make a dump specially for the shells! On the other hand, ancient oyster shells have been found in modern times in the neighbourhood. Two were found in my own garden quite near the hospital. So it may be true.

There was bull and bear baiting. The bullring was at the side of the site of the present town hall, and the inhabitants of the Mansion could watch from the balcony on the first floor which was placed there in later years. There was cock-fighting, and the Fighting Cocks, built probably about 1600, had and still has a cockpit, though today it is used for the purpose of feeding human beings. Archery was compulsory and was practised in the Long Butts behind the Tonman Ditch on the ground which is now covered by Lattimore Road and Alma Road. There were ball games, with a primitive football, hockey and golf. These were without rules, no doubt, with no holds barred, but Mulcaster, a famous educationist of Elizabeth's time, wanted to institute rules and even an umpire.

The Innholders' Guild was one of the most important, since the number of travellers of all sorts passing through St. Albans was so great that most of the roads were full of inns, which were often side by side. There were in the fifteenth century no noblemen in the town, though some important non-local people owned property. For instance, the Duke of Exeter owned the George in 1446, and let it on lease to the innkeeper. There were occasionally small gentry and some wealthy merchant families like the Attewells and the Bostocks. The mother of Abbot John of Wheathampstead was a Bostock.

Wills entered in the archdeacon's register often give a picture of the homes and clothes of those who made them. For example, in 1437 Alice Atte Welle (or Attwell) leaves to her priest a chalice, a holy water stoup, "five spones of sylver of thyke sorte that ben daylon hond and occupyed" (i.e. spoons of silver that have been daily on hand and used), "and three cusshons of work rede and grene". She also leaves a pot with small feet, a coffer "that was my mother's to lay her kerchiefs in" and a bed with a religious picture painted on it.

Legacies to her children include to her daughter Joan, "a better gown of blue with grey fur, a red belt harnessed with enamelled silver, a brass pan and a brass pot". To her daughter Alice she leaves a second better gown furred with grey, a green belt with enamelled silver fastenings, and a brass pan and a brass pot. Her sister Joan gets a blue "sengle" gown, the collar lined with satin, and another sister has a "tall gown" of blue (she evidently liked herself in blue), with a collar lined with black "bocheram", which cannot be the buckram we know. A former servant has a grey woollen dress lined with black "bocheram", and another a russet gown furred with coney. These clothes show that she was a well-to-do woman, and sufficiently important to ignore the sumptuary laws of the time, which forbade anyone under the rank of gentlewoman to wear fur. She leaves to one of the two sons, among other things, a quilt, two blankets, two pairs of sheets and a mattress. She bequeaths nine spoons of silver to be divided equally between her two sons. Her executor must have had a headache deciding just how this bequest was to be carried out.

Another will shows that the upholstery of the furniture was loose, and that there were coverlets like carpets for chairs and benches. There are many references to cushions, the word being spelt in all sorts of ways. The pots and pans were often pewter, spoons often silver, and latten (a sort of imitation brass) was used for candlesticks. One bequest of bed linen lists blankets, one white and one russet, a coverlet of green and white, and sheets of housewife's cloth, probably homespun. There is a mention of amber beads, obviously much prized.

Some of the bequests mention books. There was, of course, a great library in the Abbey, but comparatively few of the townsfolk owned books, though by the sixteenth century about half the population could read. Richard Fox, who seems to have been a sort of butler to the Abbot, left a number of books, bound and unbound. The beginnings are often given, but not, as a rule, the titles. One was a little prayer book. He left some of them to his son by description, and said that the son could also have any others he chose, but was to let two other people have some, and two volumes of the Golden Legends, which were lives of the saints, were left to the Prioress of Pré. Two of the bound books were history books, and one was a volume of foreign travel. One of the unbound books dealt with cookery, meals service and etiquette. For these particulars of wills I am indebted to an article by Dr. Owst in the *Transactions of the St. Albans Architectural and Archaeological Society*.

We do not know much about the houses in the town. Most would be timber-framed and small, but there was at least one whose importance was shown by the fact that it was a large house of stone. There are a number of documents in the city archives dealing with this Stone Hall, as it was called. It had been Abbey property, and at its first mention it was in the hands of the king and leased to Bartholomew Westby, a member of the family of Edmond, host to Henry VI in 1455, and in the years to come it passed through many hands, mostly to people described as "gentlemen". By the end of the sixteenth century it appears to have been divided and had two tenants, but by the early seventeenth century it was again in single occupation. Later on it seems to have degenerated into a tenement house, and it was still standing in 1782, but must have been pulled down soon after, since it seems to have stood where the Georgian house, now converted into offices, and called Town Hall Chambers, is situated. Some of the houses in the town were assigned to one or other of the departments of the Abbey, so that their rents went towards the upkeep. There is mention of a tenement called the Woolsack in St. Peter's Street, held of the sacristan, and the cellarer's department owned a house in Bowgate. It is said, I do not know on what authority, that Walter of Colchester, the artist of the frescoes, lived in this house instead of in the Abbey. This may be true, as he did work for other abbeys, and it may have been convenient for him to have his own establishment away from the routine of the monastery, but I am inclined to think it unlikely.

CHAPTER NINE

THE BREAK-UP OF THE ABBEY LANDS

THE break-up of the Abbey estates began immediately on the dissolution of the house. Sir Richard Lee obtained the Abbey buildings and their site, apart from the Church itself. He also acquired the manor of Squillers. At some time it had become associated with another manor, Newland, and the combined manor seems to have included all the middle of St. Albans from the High Street to St. Peter's Church. Another property acquired by Lee was the nunnery of Sopwell. Here he proceeded to pull down much of the buildings and out of them to construct a country house for himself. The great disadvantage in his eyes was that he desired to have a large park, and the public road from London passed right through the area where he was going to lay it out. This road came from Barnet via Arkley and Shenley, and continued from what is now the bottom of Mile House Lane, across the present Verulam golf-links, by the route still marked by a right-of-way to near the eastern end of Sopwell Lane, where it entered the town. Lee was a military engineer, and understood the processes of road-making, so far as it was known in his day, and so he diverted this road and constructed a new one for the people of St. Albans, the road we now call Old London Road, which joined on to a road from Hadley through South Mimms. Later on, when the St. Albans Road leading out of Barnet was cut, the Old London Road became the principal road from London, vying with the Watling Street, and the original road came to a dead end when it reached Mile House Lane, as far as wheeled traffic was concerned, and only foot-passengers kept its line alive, as they do to this day, the old road turning at an angle into Mile House Lane and joining the modern London Road. Lee also owned a house in St. Peter's Street, and from the description of the situation it would seem to be the one still existing, known as the Mansion, facing the Market Square, which is much older than its front, which itself is seventeenth century. The house known as the Stone Hall, belonging to the monastery, described in the previous chapter, was situated between Lee's house and the Moot Hall, and its position would place Lee's house just where Spencer Street now is, and Spencer Street was cut through the gardens of the Mansion. Lee is buried in St. Peter's Church.

The largest acquisition of Abbey lands was made perhaps by Ralph Rowlatt, who was a merchant of the Staple, and whose brass is in the Abbey. At his death in 1542, the inquest which enquired into his property found that he owned Gorhambury, the Pré, and the manor of Westwick, a number of houses in St. Albans, two of them in Holywell Hill and one in Fishpool Street, the manor of Sandridge, the manor of Napsbury, his own big house on Holywell Hill (Holywell House, which he built), besides the manors of Minchenbury, Barley, Caldecote, Newnham, Radwell near Baldock, all of them in Hertfordshire, and a number of areas of land, including twenty acres adjoining Holywell House, besides the advowson of several churches in the county, including Redbourn. He had two sons, Ralph junior and Amphibalus (who spells his name Amphabell; his father, in his will, called him Affabel, a most endearing variation). He had several daughters, married to scions of the most prominent citizen families, among them John Maynard (several Maynards are buried in the Abbey), and John Jennings, to whose son he left the manor of Sandridge and also Holywell House, which was to become the beloved home of his famous descendant, Sarah Jennings, Duchess of Marlborough, ancestress of Sir Winston Churchill.

His heir, Ralph the younger, became a knight and sold Gorhambury to Sir Nicholas Bacon, Lord Keeper to Queen Elizabeth the First. The house was still the twelfth-century manor house built originally by the kinsman of Abbot Geoffrey de Gorham, but had through the intervening four centuries been considerably added to, as a manuscript in Lambeth Palace library describes.

In the will of Ralph senior there is a curious clause referring to the Abbey. He asked to be buried "Yf it chaunce to be a place convenient for burial in our lady chapel within the late monastery of St. Alban where my wife lyeth and my sonne. And yf the same shalbe noo such place mete for burial than I will my body to be buried within the chapell of St. Andrew". This is intriguing. Was the Abbey not functioning three years after the Dissolution? Was it considered desecrated? The School did not, of course, occupy the Lady Chapel for another eleven years at least. St. Andrew's was the parish church adjoining the west front of the Abbey Church. When the municipality acquired the building of the Abbey Church after 1553 and made it the parish church, St. Andrew's was pulled down. The only relic of its site is the little rockery by the side of the west front.

Several other St. Albans names, which were to become very prominent, occur among the people who acquired property of the Abbey at this time. Richard Raynshaw, one of the king's sergeants of arms of the Yeomen of the Guard, obtained the Pré in 1530 from Thomas Abraham, a London merchant, who had acquired it on the fall of Wolsey. Later the king exchanged the Pré for Batchwood, and at the Dissolution the Pré was granted to Ralph Rowlatt. Raynshaw appears to have gone on living there as a tenant, since an inventory of his property when he died shows him living in a house of considerable size, with farm outbuildings. He appears to have been a very lively character, and there is a record of a complaint against him in the Star Chamber alleging that, among other disorderly actions, he had gone into the Abbey on Easter Day wearing a long sword, and accompanied by armed servants, and had ejected Ralph Rowlett from his usual pew and kept him out by force and threats, and had to be restrained by members of the congregation. Perhaps it was the result of a squabble between landlord and tenant, but we shall never know, since there is no trace of any verdict on the Star Chamber proceedings. Raynshaw is still known as the founder of the Raynshaw Charity, which supports a number of almshouses in Spicer Street. By his will he left four houses to the mayor and burgesses in trust; the rent of one of the houses, the Vine, then or later an inn, was to go to support the other three. The present almshouses were rebuilt in Victorian times, but the Vine, now an attractive private house, still survives.

A local man named Pemberton married Sir Richard Lee's daughter and inherited much of his property. It is interesting to read the enquiry which was held after her death to determine what property she held. It consisted of the manor of Sopwell with all the lands pertaining thereto—Brickfield Close, Pond Close, St. Julian's Field, Eywood Hill Field, Mill Mead, part of St. Julian's barn (why only a part?), Sopwell Mill at New Barnes, a new built house called New Barnes, and the old farmhouse called New Barnes Farmhouse, together with miscellaneous fields and odd pieces of land. Many of these names are still familiar. The family of Pemberton became well known in the seventeenth century, when Sir Goddard Pemberton was high sheriff in 1615, as was his son, Roger, five years later. Roger was the founder of the Pemberton Almshouses in the Bowgate, now the property of the city council. The legend attached says that he was out shooting with bow and arrow when an arrow accidentally killed a poor widow out gathering sticks, and in remorse he founded the almshouses for six poor widows. There is, unfortunately, no solid foundation for this picturesque story, but it would be nice to think it true. Old inhabitants will point to an arrow-head embedded above the gateway, but alas! it may have been merely a form of lightning conductor, and has been several times renewed. The Pembertons will be met with again later in the story of St. Albans.

At least one of the officials of the monastery rose to prominence after the Dissolution. This was Henry Gape, who obtained the manor of St. Michael's. He became the third mayor of St. Albans when it was granted its charter, and thenceforward, at intervals, one Gape after another held the same post, sixteen of them, right up to 1829. Members of the family, which is still represented in the city, have from time to time held office in voluntary activities, although the ancestral home of St. Michael's Manor House passed out of the possession of the family some few years ago.

Sir Thomas Wendy, physician to Henry VIII, bought Kingsbury, and became Member of Parliament for the borough. Thomas Skipwith, a son-in-law of Ralph Rowlatt, bought the Grange, a farm of the Abbey, burnt down in the 1381 revolt, and re-built. The last remnant of the property

was pulled down in 1958 to make room for a petrol station,
and nothing now remains save the name Grange Street.

The Great Gateway was not pulled down with the rest of
the conventual buildings, but became the Sessions House,
and the sessions were held there until 1631. Then it became
the gaol in place of the old Compter, next to the Town Hall,
though that still seems to have been used as a lock-up right
into the nineteenth century, according to an account of a
local riot given in a London paper in 1810. The Gateway
continued in use as a prison until a new prison was erected
at the foot of Victoria Street in 1868. The Sessions Rolls of
the Liberty of St. Albans are in the county archives and have
been calendared. They include such items as that at the
sessions in 1589 three men were sentenced to be hanged, one
for burglary, one for being a cutpurse, and one for clipping
coins. There were evidently desperate criminals in the town
in those days! At the same sessions two men arrested for
stealing cattle claimed benefit of clergy and were released.
This was a curious relic of the Middle Ages, when clergy were
the only people who could read, and they did not come under
the ordinary law, so that if a defendant claimed that he could
read, and proved it by reading a passage from the Bible, he
could not be tried by civil law but only by a church court
(which never imposed a death penalty). As time went on
the passage came to be always the same one, Psalm 51, v. 1,
and as literacy became more common, many a rogue escaped
the just reward of his sins by reading (or reciting, having
learned it from memory), the "Neck Verse". But in the same
year two men found stealing bread were whipped, and two
men and their wives were indicted as rogues and executed.

One of the duties on the shoulders of the justices in quarter
sessions was that of fixing wages. This was done at the Easter
sessions, and the rate lasted a year. There is an example of
this in the roll of 1591–2, when there is an elaborate schedule
of wages, setting out how much, for example, a mower should
get daily if he also had his food, and how much without food.
With food a mower got eightpence a day, or twelve pence
without food, a reaper had sixpence daily with food and
women reapers fivepence. No equal pay then. Eightpence
a day for skilled workers seems to have been the usual rate,

and sixpence for unskilled workers. Curiously enough, millers
and drovers of horses were paid yearly, and a distinction was
made between bachelors and married men, the former getting
forty-six shillings and eightpence yearly with a pair of boots,
but the latter fourpence daily with food.

St. Albans did not get a charter until 1553. How was
the town governed during the hiatus from 1539, when the
Abbey was dissolved? It is difficult to say, for there is no
real evidence, but a clue may perhaps be found in the arrange-
ments for the management of the Clock Tower. There is a
parcel of deeds relating to the building in the city archives,
and from these it would seem that before the Dissolution it
was in the care of trustees, of whom eighty are named in a
deed. The deed is undated, but from the names, which
include the Edmond Westby of Hall Place, who entertained
Henry VI and Margaret in 1455, it is clearly mid-fifteenth
century. In another deed dated 1 Henry VII, there are a
different lot, called feoffees, who let the building to Robert
Grave, a smith, who was to ring the bell for a quarter of an
hour between eight and nine at night and at four .in the
morning. He had to keep the clock and tenement in repair,
but not the bell nor the clapper, nor the fabric of the building.
In 1547 the feoffees granted the lease of the Clockhouse, as it
was called, to Thomas Lockey, who was probably the brother
of the first mayor six years later. The brother was one of
the feoffees, who also included Sir Richard Lee, Ralph Rowlatt,
Richard Raynshaw, Henry Gape, Thomas Skipwith, John
Maynard and John Kentish. These men would appear to
have become a sort of unofficial corporation, and it is not
stretching conjecture too far to assume that this is how local
government was carried on for the time being, for in the reign
of Elizabeth the tenancy was said to be let by "the burgesses", i.e. the mayor and corporation, who had taken the
place and powers of the feoffees.

CHAPTER TEN

ST. ALBANS BECOMES SELF-GOVERNING

THE town's first charter was dated May 12th, 1553. It defined the bounds of the town as, on the north, the New Barrys or Bars, near the modern Cricketers' public-house, the bars in Sopwell Lane on the east, that is the end farthest from Holywell Hill, Holywell House on the south, and Kingsbury Lane on the west. A common council was established of Mayor and "ten of the discreeter and better men of the said borough of Saint Alban to be Assistants and help mates to the said Mayor". The officials were to be the Steward (usually a local gentleman) a chamberlain, the sergeants at mace, two in number, and a clerk of the market. There were to be two Members of Parliament to represent the borough. The charter also gave the right to have a gaol, two markets (represented by the cattle market now closed and the Saturday market), and three fairs, with, as before, a Court of Pie Powder, the court of summary jurisdiction which dealt with offences committed in the market without waiting for an ordinary sitting of the justices. A separate commission of the peace was set up, the descendant of the Abbot's Liberty, and the Mayor and Steward were to be justices. The Liberty of St. Albans continued, but as a division of the county, and had its own quarter sessions until the nineteenth century, when it was separated from the borough court, which from that time has not had a court of quarter sessions of its own.

This charter was confirmed at the end of the same year by Queen Mary I, but the original of this confirmation is not extant. Both charters were confirmed by Elizabeth I in 1560 (1559 Old Style), and she later granted another charter, usually called the Wine Charter, which gave power to the corporation to license two people to sell wine in the town. The proceeds of the licences were to go to the support of the School and for the master's salary. James I increased the number of wine licences to three, still for the benefit of the

School. The fairs at Michaelmas and Lady Day in time became pleasure fairs, and the St. Albans Day fair was a horse fair. These fairs were abolished in 1873.

After the Dissolution the trade of the town became mainly catering for travellers. There had been, as in every other mediaeval town, a number of craft guilds, but by the time of Elizabeth I they had grouped themselves into four, the innholders, mercers, shoemakers, and victuallers. In 1662 they were reduced to two, the innholders and mercers, and they disappeared after 1834.

The religious changes under Mary did not affect the town much. There is no record of any local person suffering death for his faith in the town of the first British martyr. George Tankerfield, who was burnt in Romeland, was brought from Barnet for the purpose, as a warning which was apparently not needed. Perhaps the scepticism rife in the town during the last years of the monastery had survived to cause a certain indifference towards religion which enabled the citizens to anticipate the later Vicar of Bray.

By the time of Elizabeth I, Gorhambury had changed hands as already stated. It had been bought from the Rowlatts by a distant relative, Sir Nicholas Bacon, Lord Keeper of the Privy Seal, and from then the Bacon family became the outstanding influence in the town for many years. Bacon pulled down the old house and built a new home on a different site. He became High Steward of the Liberty and took a great interest in the School, which still possesses books given by him. He made new rules for the school which read oddly today. The boys were to attend at the stroke of six in the morning from March to September, and at seven from September to March. They were to stop at eleven for dinner and go on again from one o'clock until five in the afternoon. There were not to be more than a hundred and twenty boys on roll. In 1596, one Angell, a carpenter, whose family finally ceased to be tradesmen in the town only recently, was paid to put up a hundred pegs for the boys' hats. The scholars were not to be absent for more than three days without good excuse under threat of expulsion, and the schoolmaster himself was not to be away more than six days at a time, and not more than thirty days in all during the year. The time for play was at the discretion of the master and not more than once a week, except by special permission of the governors. The parents had to provide ink, paper, wax candles for winter, a bow, three arrows, bow-strings, with shooting glove and bracer.

The accounts of the School, which are extant, are most interesting. In 1591—"Paid to Campion the glazier for mending the windows broken by rude boys in the time of divine service". Windows constantly gave trouble, as today. We read in 1603, "Received of Mr. Gibson, the Schoolmaster, towards the charge of the glass windows, the which he collected of the parents whose sons did break the same windows". Modern teachers will be interested to know how much was paid to supply teachers in 1601. "Paid to one Mr. Collins for teaching in the school in the absence of the usher . . . 6s. 8d.". Even the headmaster's salary was not too secure, for in 1603 occurs the following: "Item, borrowed of Mr. Mayor to pay Mr. Gibson the Schoolmaster, 20s." The salary at that time had just been put up from £20 per annum to £22. Gibson's successor was James Shirley, the poet, but he stayed only two years. Perhaps the young hopefuls of St. Albans were too much for him. Boys are not kind to poets. The salary rose very slowly (as is the habit with teachers' salaries), and it was not until 1694 that the head received as much as £30 and the usher (assistant master), £24.

The examination bogey existed even in the seventeenth century, and there are references to examiners and governors. Each year two members of the council were chosen to be governors, and to this day the Mayor is a governor, *ex officio*, and there are three other representatives of the council on the body of governors. In 1629 there is a very interesting entry in the records: "Paid at the taverne for wyne when the gentlemen met about jotting downe the method of teaching of the scholars . . . iiis. ivd."

Governors and examiners were entertained to a meal when they visited the school. There is such an entry in 1616, "Payd to Antony Selliock" (the landlord of the Red Lion) "the 29th May for the diett for the examiners . . . xiis.". And a still more interesting note for 1633, "Imprimis, spent upon the visiters of the school and upon Mr. John Harmer, schoolmaster, and Mr. Richard Goddard, usher of the same schole, a little before Christmas 1633, when the schollers broke up schools in wine the some of iis. iiid.".

Bacon's fine new house was honoured within four years by a visit from his royal mistress. She was not impressed, and remarked disconcertingly, "My Lord, what a little house you have gotten". But Sir Nicholas, with great presence of mind and wit answered, "Madam, my house is well, but it is you that have made me too big for my house". It may be noted in passing that Sir Nicholas was of ample build. But he had noted her opinion, and when she came next she found that he had added a long gallery to the house. As it was a hundred and twenty feet long, one hopes that she was satisfied. The beautiful windows of English enamelled glass on show at Gorhambury today probably came from this gallery. The accounts are still in existence of the cost of the Queen's third visit. Beer and ale cost nearly £27, wine £57 5s. 8d., lighting £15 18s., poultry £105 7s. 11d., fish £36 18s. 6d., the cook brought from London specially for the occasion cost £12, and the total bills which Bacon had to meet came to £577 6s. 7¼d. On one of her visits she was presented with a loyal address by the Mayor, who is supposed to have been living in the Mansion in St. Peter's Street at the time.

It was in the year 1577 that Richard Raynshaw died. There is a most interesting inventory of the contents of his house, drawn up by his executors, of whom Ralph Maynard, buried in the Abbey, was one. It gives a picture of a large house. We read of the gilden parlour, the great parlour, the old parlour, the French chamber, the great new chamber, Mr. Raynshaw's chamber, the middle chamber, besides a chamber over the kitchen, which seems to have been a sort of storeroom and contained dishes, saucers, candlesticks, and so on, a kitchen, a buttery, besides bakehouse, brewhouse, milkhouse, wellhouse and larder. The rooms were well, even luxuriously, furnished. Some of the curtains were of silk, and there were plenty of cushions. There was a carpet in the old parlour, and a good many court cupboards. There were six bedsteads of panelled wood, each with its feather bed and bolsters. But there is a surprising lack of chairs, only six being mentioned. Tables were of two sorts, those which were trestles with what are termed "frames", and joined tables, those which could not be taken down. Forms were provided for sitting at meals; only in the great parlour is there any suggestion of a fireplace, and there a pair of andirons, a fire shovel and a pair of tongs were provided. The ladies of the household beautified the furnishings, for there were six cushions of needlework, though they were said to be old, and two of crewelwork. Other cushions were covered in silk, others were in red and green, three in red and three in blue and yellow, and one very grand cushion in crimson satin embroidered in gold. The three executors were all men, and that perhaps explains some of the omissions. For instance, there are only seven blankets listed and three coverlets. There is, however, a long list of bed and table linen and the value is extremely high. Seven pairs of linen sheets are valued at six pounds, and five pair of another texture, called towen, were worth five pounds. There were eight long linen table-cloths and six of an inferior type. There was "a fair damask tablecloth" with ten damask table napkins, and a damask towel (obviously used for wiping the hands at the table) and a set of diaper linen cloth, twelve napkins and a towel. There were four dozen "flaxen" napkins, perhaps of coarse linen, with two dozen "towe" napkins, these probably for everyday use with the more inferior tablecloths. Bed linen included eight pillowcases and six of a poorer kind with five towels. The kitchen seems to have been well equipped, with pots and pans of brass and utensils like dripping pans, spice mortar, ladles, spit, frying pan, trivet, and pothooks and hangers. The buttery contained candlesticks, basins, platters and dishes, fruit dishes, and saucers, with a carved wooden cupboard in which to keep them.

Mr. Raynshaw was somewhat of a dandy and spent lavishly on his clothes, which were surprisingly expensive, though obviously the executors did not list all his wearing apparel, since there is no mention of underclothes or of shoes and boots. And there are only two pairs of hose. But he had a damask gown "furred" with satin which was worth £6 13s. 4d., an equivalent of at least £150 in our money. His grosgrain gown was worth £4, and two cloth gowns, though old, were valued at forty shillings. A satin coat at £3, and a jerkin of grosgrain, cheap at thirteen shillings and fourpence, with a cloth coat at six shillings and eightpence, two doublets of satin and fustian, at thirteen shillings and fourpence, completed the list. His table must have glittered when fully set out. He had a basin and ewer of silver worth £15, and some piece difficult to decipher of silver-gilt, worth the enormous sum of £24; there was a standing cup with cover, double-gilt, a goblet of similar metal, a silver salt with cover double-gilt, a plain bowl and another silver salt, both "parcel-gilt", two dozen silver spoons worth £6, and six other silver spoons somewhat less valuable, and a little goblet of silver, cheap at twenty-six shillings and eightpence. We do not know what jewellery he had. Three pieces are mentioned, a chain, a signet ring and a ring with a solitaire emerald, all gold, but they are not valued, as they had been given away in the will. Even his creditors and debtors are listed. The "good debts" include one of £25 due from Sir Ralph Rowlatt and the "desperate debts" (a delightful term) include £4 owing from Francis Ferris of Brockett Hall, and three smaller debts from St. Albans men.

This inventory is on a long strip of parchment about five inches wide and some yards long, which is in the archives of the St. Albans City Council.

The Elizabethan charter, which confirmed the previous charters, made provision for filling vacancies on the council. When one of the ten assistants died, someone else was to be appointed by the rest to take his place. Once appointed he could not be turned out. Later the custom arose of appointing twenty-four assistants, who came to be called councillors, and the original ten became known as principal assistants and later on aldermen.

The Mayor held the office of clerk of the market, and fixed the price of bread, ale and victuals. One example of the control of such goods occurs in the minutes of June 10th, 1588, when several people were brought up for brewing "extraordinary strong ale", and were reprimanded. The corporation minutes begin in 1586 and are fascinating reading. They record, *inter alia*, elections of freemen. Freemen had the sole right of voting and of doing business in the town. Eldest sons of freemen had the right to become freemen in their turn, but strangers had to pay twenty pounds or more, and this was a fertile source of corruption in the eighteenth century. They paid because they wanted to trade in the town, and at first the right to vote was of no importance. It became of primary consideration in the days of bribery, and we shall meet instances later on. Here is an example of the admission of a stranger freemen in 1588. The warden of the Mercers' Company reported William Barber for dealing in flax, he not being a freeman. He was granted his freedom in consideration of his taking and bringing up one of the children of a widow of the town until it became self-supporting.

The minutes cast many sidelights on the state of the town in the days of Elizabeth I. At this same council meeting a sum of eight pounds was taken out of the town's chest to pay for looms and other equipment for weaving, and it was stated that a Dutchman had been brought to St. Albans to instruct the poor of the town in the arts of spinning and worsted weaving. This Dutchman, Anthony Moner, came in 1588. A note is made that the purchases consisted of "a new great loom and two flayers, one for silk and the other for cruell and all that belonged to them, at a cost of three pounds fifteen shillings; two little looms, one for silk the other cruell, twenty-one shillings; seven wheels, thirty-six shillings; wheels to wind yarn, twenty pence; three blades, sixteen pence; things to lay on warp, eightpence; warping pins and four dozen quills, six shillings; one hartle, eightpence; and a pair of combs, fifteen shillings". And at the September meeting, the Mayor was ordered to search his own ward to see how many children of the poor might be taught by Moner. In November, Thomas Woolley was given ten pounds taken from the chest to buy wool to give out to the Dutchman in instalments, the latter to pay for each lot when he fetched the next. There is a note that when the ten pounds had been taken out there was five pounds and some odd money left in the chest. In 1589 an agreement was made with Moner that he should teach four men to comb and dress wool, in addition to teaching the children. This is an early example of both the welfare state and municipal enterprise.

We grumble at litter nowadays, but our refuse collectors do not have to cope with such things as the following extracts relate: "1587; Middle Ward. Five people made a dunghill in Market Place to the annoyance of the inhabitants." Surely an understatement! In the same year: "Two people made a dunghill in Dagnall Lane before the Council Chamber and were ordered to remove same." In 1588: "Philip Grene was ordered to remove logs which he had laid in the Malt Market, or pay fourpence if he did not remove the nuisance within seven days." And again in 1588: "In Fishpool Ward, a baker was fined for laying a dead horse in Dagnall Lane."

Poor Dagnall Street! Ten years later the litterbugs were still at it. Matthew Davis laid timber and dung in Dagnall Lane and several others were reported for a like offence. In 1612 some men were summoned for putting timber logs and dunghills in the streets and digging pits in St. Peter's Street. In the following year there is an entry that, unless the bailiffs cause the dunghills made about the Market House and Market Cross to be cleared away before the next night, they should forfeit three shillings and fourpence, and an entry in 1620 reports that Hugh Spencer, a baker, made a heap of dung before the house of Mrs. Sara Rowbotham in St. Peter's Street. The lady survived the unpleasantness for nine years and was buried in St. Peter's Church.

With streets in such a state it is little wonder that the minutes are full of references to prominent citizens being reported for putting posts and rails in front of their houses, the object being no doubt to keep a little space of greater cleanliness, but this was against the town's regulations obviously, for they were all fined, though some of them managed to keep the fencing. Roger Pemberton was one of those who fenced in the front of his house in St. Peter's Street; it was probably on the east side, not far from the corner of Shropshire Lane, perhaps right on the corner. All the indications are that St. Albans was both untidy and smelly in the days of Elizabeth the First.

Sometimes the punishments were fines, sometimes a period in the stocks or pillory. The pillory stood permanently in the Shambles, the stretch of the Market Place between Timothy White's shop today and the Clock Tower. The stocks were on wheels and were moved to various places in the town, according to where the authorities thought they might present the best lesson when an offender was receiving punishment.   They were kept in the Counter House or Compter, which was part of the premises of the Moot Hall.   The latter was by this time generally known as the Council Chamber;   later on, it was called the Town Hall, which name it retained until the erection of the later building, which, incidentally, was misnamed town hall, as it belonged partly to the county and not to the city.   It is to be hoped that in the not far distant future, there will be a Town Hall really belonging to the city in the civic centre.

Apart from the constant and ever-growing traffic through the town—how history repeats itself—St. Albans had no great importance during the later Tudor times, so that one event stands out in our civic history, as it does in national history—the coming of the Armada.   In 1588, when invasion threatened, the Queen sent to Hertfordshire for a bodyguard of five hundred men, and some of these came from St. Albans. Fifty-two of our trainband were sent to Tilbury, and mention of their equipment is to be found in the corporation minutes under the date July 8th, 1588.   So some St. Albans men heard that historic speech at Tilbury, and probably talked about it for the rest of their lives.

When, each May, a number of candidates endeavour to win or retain a seat on the council, they might be amused (or amazed) to learn that their fellow citizens of the sixteenth and seventeenth centuries were not nearly so eager to become councillors.   Over and over again in the records there are such entries as in 1590, when Gilbert Wells was elected a chief burgess, but as he refused to serve he was fined £5, a very heavy fine.   The following year, a vacancy having arisen, John Porter was chosen in his absence.   On his return he refused to serve.   He was fined £5, but refused to pay the fine, so he was committed to prison and another election was held, of course, by the council only.   William Antrobus was chosen;   he, too, refused to take office at first, but later weakened and asked time to consider.   He was given till next morning, when he reiterated his refusal, and was committed to prison until the fine was paid.   So now there were two men in prison.   The same night two friends of the prisoners came forward at a meeting with the council at the Christopher, and went surety that the money would be paid by agreed dates. Three years later Gilbert Wells, who had refused office in 1590, had still not paid his fine, and was brought before the court, where he pleaded that he was not anything like as well off as people thought him, but was considerably in debt, so he was excused half the fine. We are not told whether he did eventually pay up.

Even the members of the council did not always obey the regulations, about clean streets, for example. Robert Shrimpton, the old gentleman who used to tell the story of what he had seen while the Abbey was still in being, was Mayor in 1588, 1596 and 1605, yet he was reported at least once because the channel in front of his Holywell Hill house was neglected and needed repair. The very next month an alehouse keeper lost his licence because he permitted the servants of Mr Shrimpton and Mr. Lockey (another councillor and ex-Mayor) to "play and banquet" in his house during service on Sunday. Both these councillors were absent from a meeting of the corporation in 1591 after warning, and were fined two shillings each, but the fine was returned to them. Later on in the same year, Shrimpton did the same thing and was again fined two shillings, of which one shilling was returned to him. With the other shilling the council treated themselves, and met at the Christopher that evening. In the August, Lockey "did with opprobrious words, abuse himself towards Mr. Mayor and the burgesses in the council chamber". He was fined twenty shillings and had to make a public apology.

These fines for absence were in accordance with a decision made that, as the principal burgesses had absented themselves very frequently for the past two years, in future if anyone should absent himself three times following he should lose his place or else be heavily fined. On several occasions it is recorded that certain members of the council used unseemly words and abuse to the Mayor, and were fined.

Because a councillor once appointed normally sat for life, we sometimes meet with such a case as the old man who was becoming senile. One such "hath cutt his gowne and for a longe time hath been crasie and infirm in mind". At the same meeting it was noted that two had grown old and feeble.

Even as late as 1698 there occurred the curious misdeed of a councillor cutting his gown as a sign of contempt for the council. On the same day as he was fined, an alderman was fined a further forty shillings for having "uttered false and base reports and reflections upon the Mayor and Aldermen". In those days one had to be very respectful to Mr. Mayor and the corporation. Under the same rules there would have been many people fined in my youth, when the city council was derisively known as "the forty thieves". Even today it has been known for some people not to be wholly respectful in what they say about the corporation, though I must admit from personal experience that they are punctiliously kind to the Mayor.

The records of the old archdeaconry throw some light on the standard of work of the new clergy, who had taken the place of the pre-Reformation incumbents. There are many accounts of visitations and documents dealing with the learning of these men, and there appear to have been a good many unlearned clergy. From the volumes dealing with the years 1588 to 1622, one may find lists of "inferior sort of Ministers", and they include Thomas Weatherhead, Vicar of St. Michael's, and Richard Lightfoote, Vicar of St. Stephen's. In 1586 several of these were examined, and Lightfoote is noted as having passed his test. "Learned Preachers" were appointed as examiners, one of whom was Roger Williams, B.D., Parson of St. Albans, that is, incumbent of the Abbey Church. A year or so later Mr. Lightfoote was reported to be preaching "painfully and diligently in his own parish". The word "painfully" has a slightly sinister sound, and leads to speculation as to how his sermons struck his congregation.

A return of 1588 is most outspoken. Weatherhead was by now eighty years of age, and a deacon preached for him. The Vicar of Hexton was said to be "an olde sickly man and no preacher". William More of St. Peter's was stated to be "no preacher, neither hath he used any great diligence in preaching. . . . He hath been detected for his slackness in catechising and for his slackness in performing his exercises". As a result he was under suspension.

There are not many allusions to the health of the town in the sixteenth century, but there are some entries showing that the plague sometimes came to the citizens. On July 12th, 1625, a shilling was paid to the town clerk for drawing up orders about the plague, and a pesthouse was set up and attendants appointed to assist the sufferers. A curious touch is given by the fact that fears of the plague were so great that if a stranger died suddenly, poor widows were engaged to search the body to see if there were any sign of plague! We do not know what the poor widows thought about this callous willingness to sacrifice them.

Entries in parish registers of baptisms, weddings and deaths were made compulsory from 1538, and give a picture of an immense amount of infantile mortality. When a baptism is followed within a few days by a death it is fairly certain that it was a baby who died. Smallpox carried off many people. In St. Peter's parish alone, in eight months ending February 1711, there were twenty-nine deaths from smallpox. And there was an outbreak of plague in 1604. We know this from a legal action in 1608, which concerned a certain Thomas Woolley, a member of a well-known family in St. Albans. In that year he filed a bill in Chancery against Thomas Wells, probably son of the Gilbert Wells, an innkeeper, who refused to sit on the council. Woolley said that he had had a convenient dwelling-place in St. Albans until the plague killed three of his sons. One of them, a trader, had stocks of goods in his house when he died, and Thomas let the house to a man who bought the stock. Since then Thomas had been destitute and unprovided with a convenient dwelling-house, though he said he was "the most ancient principal burgess". Then he tried to get hold of the Chequers Inn in the Malt Market by a reversion when the existing tenant's lease expired. This belonged to a brother living in Essex. Wells went to see this brother secretly and bought the property, his alleged reason being that he already owned the adjoining inn, the Half Moon. He offered a lease to Woolley and then withdrew the offer on the ground that he wanted to safeguard his windows from buildings which Woolley might add to the Chequers. It is obvious that his real reason was to stop competition, and it shows how many inns there were, some even being next door to each other.

It was somewhat impudent for Woolley to claim that he

was destitute, for he belonged to one of the wealthiest families in the town. Actually he died in that same year, and his will shows that he had a house in the Vintry, he owned the Boar's Head in the Malt Market, the Horsehead on Holywell Hill, the Crane and the Half Moon (he had evidently managed to buy it from Wells, after all), and in addition was lord of the manor of Harpsfield (now covered by the Hawker Siddeley Aerodrome) and of the manor of Plentyes in Stopsley, Luton. There was also a brewer's business in the family. It is hardly the picture of a destitute man, but perhaps the description was merely legal fiction.

The Lady Chapel, St. Albans Abbey.

CHAPTER ELEVEN

SIR FRANCIS BACON

SIR NICHOLAS BACON died in 1579, and his estates passed to his son Anthony, the elder son of his second marriage. Anthony was an invalid and died in 1601 without children, so the property was inherited by the younger brother, Francis. He was an amazing man and the most interesting character of the early seventeenth century in St. Albans. He was once summed up as "the wisest, brightest, meanest of mankind", but it is doubtful whether this facile judgment is fair or true. He certainly was brilliantly clever. In an age when undergraduates at the universities were considerably younger than today, and Wolsey earned the nickname of "the Boy Bachelor" at fifteen, Bacon went up to Cambridge at eleven years of age. At fourteen he was admitted to Gray's Inn as a law student, and a year later went to Paris on the staff of the English Ambassador, being intended for the diplomatic service. But his father died and there was no longer the money for this, so he returned to England and went on with his law studies, becoming a barrister at twenty-one. Then he entered Parliament. Curiously enough, he obtained no preferment in the reign of Elizabeth, because he was, as a boy, a favourite of the queen when she visited his parents, but in the reign of James I he gained spectacular promotion, ending up in 1618 as Lord Chancellor and Baron Verulam. Three years later he was made Viscount St. Albans, but few call him that nowadays; to St. Albans he is for ever Sir Francis Bacon, our most famous fellow-Albanian.

But on his way up he made powerful enemies, and he did not help matters by his somewhat questionable methods. In his home at Gorhambury, which he loved with a fierce devotion, he was the great man. The historian Aubrey wrote: "When he was at his country house at Gorhambury, St. Albans seemed as if the court were there, so nobly did he live." His magnificence roused jealousy, and the great Duke of

Buckingham was in the forefront of his enemise. In 1621 he was accused in Parliament of bribery and corruption. These malpractices sound today much worse than they did to his contemporaries three hundred and forty years ago, when it was taken for granted that judges were sweetened by presents, and corruption was a part of everyday life. The whole business reeks of intrigue in high places. Bacon was condemned to go to the Tower, to pay a fine of £40,000, and not to hold any office of state again. But here the king stepped in. Bacon's stay in the Tower lasted only two or three days, and the Crown never claimed the fine, leaving Bacon indebted to the king for that sum. It had the effect of getting him out of his financial difficulties to a certain degree, for his extravagance was enormous. He seems never to have been able to manage his finances, and he was in debt everywhere. But while he owed the king money, no one else could step in to force money from him. Every one of his debtors had to wait until the king was paid, and in the event they waited for the rest of his life, and then found that his affairs were in such a tangle that his executors in despair threw in their hands and refused to try to sort things out, preferring to resign.

After his disgrace Bacon retired to Gorhambury, where he refused to sell any timber to help him out of his difficulties, saying that he would not sell his feathers. He employed his enforced leisure studying history, science and philosophy, writing books and essays, and planning a beautiful garden. One of his most charming essays is that "On Gardens", where he says that the ideal size of a garden is thirty acres! But in those days labour was cheap, and we need not stretch our imagination to fancy him digging and weeding with his own hands.

He had married the daughter of a wealthy London merchant, but she did not relish the idea of sharing a house with the Lady Anne, his mother, to whom Sir Nicholas had left the house for her lifetime. She steadily became more eccentric, and one report speaks of her as "frantick". She had always been a most possessive mother, worrying her son in her letters with details of what he should wear and how he should take care of himself, as if he were a child instead of a distinguished statesman, and it is little wonder that her daughter-in-law jibbed at living with her. So Francis built himself a new house near some ponds not far from Shafford Bridge to satisfy the fashionable craving for ornamental waters in gardens. He designed the house himself, and there is in existence a drawing of it which shows that it was a most unusual building. The construction was not well carried out, and it was a constant source of expense in the way of repairs, so much so that, when he died, his heir had no desire to live there, and within a few years it had been sold to a local carpenter for £400, who pulled it down and sold the materials and cleared the ground so completely that, although the ponds are still there, all trace of the house has vanished.

He was a great lawyer, he was a great writer, he was an historian, but perhaps above all he was, as J. G. Crowther described him, a philosopher of science. His *Novum Organum* pointed the way to a new scientific outlook, to the importance of proving any opinion by experiment. He was, in a sense, the founder of the Royal Society for the Advancement of Science, though he was dead years before it began. His scientific curiosity led to his death. He was driving to Highgate on a visit when a snowstorm was raging, and it occurred to him that possibly cold might arrest decay in food. So he stopped his coach, bought a chicken from a cottager, and set to work to stuff it with snow. Unfortunately he became very chilled during this experiment in refrigeration, and had to stop at a friend's house in Highgate. His friend was absent from home, but the housekeeper, thrilled at the advent of so distinguished a guest, put him into the best bedroom, which was unaired, and as a result Bacon died. He is probably buried in St. Michael's Church, as he stated in his will, "For my burial, it may be in St. Michael's Church. There was my mother buried, and it is the parish church of my mansion house of Gorhambury, and it is the only Christian Church within the walls of Old Verulam. I would have the charge of my funeral not to exceed three hundred pounds at most". The position of the tomb is unknown. His marriage had not been a happy one, and before he died he had added a codicil to his will, stating that his wife was to have "nothing but her right", and it is a fact that she remarried within a matter of days after his death. This may explain the absence of knowledge of the whereabouts of his body. His heir was the husband of a niece, Sir Thomas Meautys, who had acted as his secretary, and he set up a very fine and unusual statue of Bacon in the chancel of the church, showing him sitting in a chair, either musing or asleep.

He left very heavy debts totalling something like the equivalent of a quarter of a million pounds at present value. Among his creditors were many of his employees, and there is a list of these debts among the Gorhambury papers. They show that Richard Wood was owed £50 for two and a half years' wages; Henry Smith, who was the bailiff, was owed £38; David Omount, the cook, £30; William Sears, the coachman, £10; and John Abraham, the footman, £11 for wages and a suit of apparel. As was previously stated the executors, faced with such a tangle, refused to carry out their duties, and poor Meautys found himself compelled to let Gorhambury furnished for some years.

It may be well to mention the suggestion that Bacon might have been the author of the plays attributed to Shakespeare. His own writings disprove this. He was a fine and polished prose writer, but he was no poet. His own verses are the best proof of that. As J. G. Crowther, the author of *Bacon, the First Statesman of Science*, says, "the volume and profundity of Bacon's political, scientific and prose works are so great, that it is really too much to suggest that he wrote all Shakespeare, too".

CHAPTER TWELVE

SEVENTEENTH-CENTURY ST. ALBANS

UNTIL the outbreak of the civil war, St. Albans went on its quiet and uneventful way. When the citizens discussed the doings of king and parliament, feeling was mainly for parliament. No doubt news was disseminated by the crews and passengers of the numerous coaches which drew up at the equally numerous inns.

We find a few interesting items in the council records. In 1619, five butchers' stalls were leased to Widow Harvey and her son for twenty-one years at twenty shillings per annum. This gives us the long-term stallage rate, and gives a glimpse of a feminine forerunner of the multiple store. In July 1629 the Mayor sat as clerk of the market, and fixed the price of wine as follows: "Claret and white wine at 8d. the quart, Kanarie wine at 1s. 2d. the quart, Muscadell at 1s. the quart, Malligo wine 1s. the quart, and sherrie wine at 1s. the quart." Fortunately, there is a note that greater or lesser measures were to cost in proportion, else we might wonder what the condition of our predecessors might have been after the consumption of wine by the quart! In 1638 comes the first mention of the mayoral allowance for expenses. At the November meeting it was resolved that as previous mayors "had sustained verie greate charges" during their mayoralties, and as their successors were "most likelie to sustayne yerelie more and greater charges, troubles, losses and expenses . . . than heretofore they have done, by reason of the greate changes of the tymes that now are, and hereafter are likelie to ensue", £32 a year should be granted to Ralph Pemberton, the current Mayor, and to his successors, over and above the sum of forty shillings which was allowed to the Mayor for distribution in charity to strangers, and the thirty shillings yearly allowed towards the "charge of his dyet" at the Court of Record, and the £3 the bailiffs paid him from the profits of the fairs and markets.

The Mayor's Accounts are in existence for a large number of years and are fascinating reading. As they became more formalised it would appear that the Mayor kept a careful account of all the moneys he expended in the course of his duties, and that these were added up and the Mayor recompensed for his out-of-pocket expenses, these accounts being audited by two of the aldermen. One of the documents records that in 1641 Anne Goldsmith left twenty pounds for the poor to trustees who included the Mayor, and a lady with the delightful name of "Fromabove Dove".

The quarrels between the king and parliament grew ever more serious, and their effects were felt even in quiet St. Albans. The king demanded the payment of shipmoney from inland towns, and our citizens bitterly resented the exaction, but we had no Hampden to fight this battle for us, though a petition was presented to parliament, complaining about the methods adopted by the high sheriff, Sir Thomas Coningsby, in its collection. The Mayor, William Newe, received proclamations from both sides, and being a royalist he put forward those of the king. He was summoned before the bar of the House of Commons to give his excuses, and these not proving satisfactory, he was sent to the Fleet Prison. When he was released he considered that the expenses of his imprisonment were part of reasonable mayoral expenses, and charged them to the town, but was speedily disabused of this idea by the council.

St. Albans was a centre of recruiting for the parliamentary army. One of the active local gentlemen was Colonel Alban Cox, of Beaumonds (or Beaumonts). His house was where the Marlborough Buildings now stand. He was a personal friend of Oliver Cromwell, who stayed with him in St. Albans several times. Cox undertook the training of the cavalry force raised in the town, which became a part of the force of the Earl of Essex. His army of about two thousand men arrived at St. Albans in August 1642 on their way to Edgehill. We find an allusion to the battle in the churchwardens' accounts of St. Peter's, where the entry occurs, "Paid to a soldier that came from Edgehill, 5s.". Later on, Essex made the town the headquarters of his army, which was poorly disciplined, and the pillory was made movable so that it could be set up in the parts of the town where the army was billeted.

Henry Meautys, the owner of Gorhambury, had let the house for a year to the Earl of Sussex, and Lady Sussex wrote to Essex asking for protection from the soldiers for her and "my good olde Lord". This was granted, whereupon, Lady Sussex, satisfied, is said to have gone off to London on a spending spree.

The gentry of Hertfordshire then joined with other eastern counties to set up a Parliamentary Council of War for these eastern counties, and the Herts members included Robert Cecil of Hatfield, the Mayor of St. Albans, the two Pemberton brothers, Henry Meautys, and John Rowbotham, a member of another prominent St. Albans family. He was a relative of the lady who had been annoyed by the litter-louts some twenty years earlier.

One eventful day in 1643 the high sheriff, greatly daring, rode into the town with a small troop, and from the steps of the Eleanor Cross read a proclamation calling out the militia for the king. The crowd which gathered must have been laughing at his temerity and his optimism, when there was a stir at the back, and round the corner from Holywell Hill a body of horsemen was riding towards them, and at the head was Cromwell. A skirmish followed in the High Street, the sheriff was forced to take refuge in an innyard, probably the Red Lion, where he was eventually captured, and later sent to London to the Tower. It is fair to say, however, that not all his audience were against him, and that Cromwell had to wait for a small reinforcement before he could get into the innyard to capture the bold royalist.

Expecting, with our nearness to London, that we might see another Battle of St. Albans, the citizens betook themselves to improving the defences of the town. Trenches were dug and earthworks raised, the works being specially strong near St. Peter's Church and at the St. Stephen's end of the town. In the Mayor's Accounts under the date of 1642-3, there appears the entry, "Paid to three men for six days work done at the townes end for mending up of the forts there at the rate of 10d. a day ... 5s. For two men's work more for three days work at St. Peters Street end 3s. 4d.".

By the end of 1643 there was a great army lying round and in St. Albans, hungry and discontented. They were on

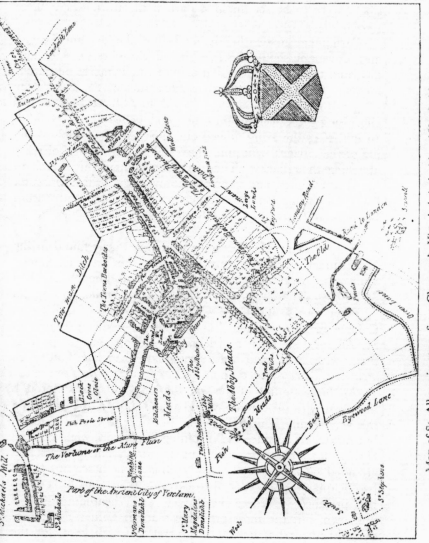

Map of St. Albans in 1700, from Chauncy's *Historical Antiquities of Hertfordshire*.

the point of mutiny, for they had received no wages for some time. They were also badly fed, and in November the weather turned snowy. It is about this time that we are told that the stocks were to be set up in a part of the town where there were soldiers.

Parliament made the demand that the Solemn League and Covenant should be read in all churches on a certain day, and the parishioners sign or make their marks on parchments. In the churchwardens' accounts of St. Peter's for 1643–4 there is this entry: "Paid to Gilbert Spencer for engrossing the Covenant into the parchment roll . . . 2s. 6d.". In mid-1644 the army moved out of St. Albans, much to the joy of the citizens, who must have taken a deep sigh of relief at seeing their backs. They went on a disastrous march to the West Country, and some notes, now in the British Museum, found in the pocket of a soldier at Lostwithiel, end, "from Bodmin to Lostwithiel and from thence, like rogues, to ye Divell".

A good many Hertfordshire men were to be found in the New Model Army of Cromwell. After the Battle of Naseby some of the royalist prisoners, on their way to London, reached St. Albans. There were more prisoners converging on London by other routes, and there was such a hold-up of traffic that Colonel Fiennes was told "to stay all the soldier prisoners at St. Albans" till further orders. St. Albans had to provide them with food, and was very glad when the bottleneck yielded and they passed on.

At the beginning of the war the king had passed through the town with all ceremony and pomp, but in 1646 he came this way again. This time he did not dare to enter the town, but turned off outside, and, avoiding St. Albans, went through byways to Wheathampstead, no longer in kingly dress and attended by a retinue, but pretending to be a servant to his two chaplains, and reduced to carrying their bags to keep up the pretence. Where he stayed at Wheathampstead is unknown, but the most probable place is Lamer Park, now demolished, and if he did the secret was well kept, for the Garrards did not lose their property or suffer any punishment. By 1647 relations between the army and parliament were becoming very strained, and Cromwell wrote from Royston that unless the soldiers were paid their wages he would march on the capital. Following this, the army began to move south, and on the way arrived at St. Albans. There the leaders were met by representatives of the City of London Corporation, who made appeasing speeches, were fed well and departed. A few days later, a month's pay was sent from London, but with a demand that the army should move to at least forty miles from the capital, which they did on June 24th. Once again St. Albans heaved a sigh of relief.

Yet again, however, they had to cope with a large body of men, this time prisoners from the siege of Colchester. The news arrived that a ragged army of hungry, wounded prisoners was on its way, and the citizens, to whom all honour be paid for their humanity, rose to the occasion. They set aside St. Peter's Church for the reception of the men, taking out all the windows, as much to secure ventilation as for safety to the glass, and then they levied a tax on themselves to buy food and medical supplies.

After the execution of the king, there is a note in the Mayor's Accounts, "Paid to James Campion for taking down the King's arms in the Glass Window of the Town Hall and setting up other glass in the place of it". St. Albans seems to have taken the austerities of the Commonwealth period philosophically. Several of the local clergy were evicted, including the Rector of the Abbey Church, but there is no mention in the council minutes of anything exciting happening in the wider world. St. Albans, however, was cured of its opposition to the monarchy, and when General Monk, who had been in command of the army in Scotland, marched down through England towards London, having opened negotiations with Charles II in Breda, he was received with delirious enthusiasm by the people of St. Albans when he arrived on a January market day, to stay five days. During this time he met delegations from the various parts of the county, and received petitions that the king should return. Some months later the town celebrated the restoration of Charles; bonfires and boisterous merrymaking kept the citizens awake, and the drinking of sack at the Market Cross broke all records. The corporation stood treat to the citizens, and so did the innkeepers and private well-to-do Albanians.

Mrs. Selioke, the licensee of the Red Lion, took three pounds eleven shillings for wine and tobacco, quaintly said to be "Drunk when our Sovereign Lord Charles the Second was proclaimed king". There are many similar accounts mentioned, and payment for broken pots and pitchers is also remarked upon. St. Albans must have suffered from a monstrous collective hangover the next morning.

In 1664, Charles granted a new charter to the town, and the title of Principal Burgess was changed to alderman. A very interesting entry in the corporation records refers to the precautions against fire. Some years before, it had been noted that "Many sudden fires had happened to the undoing of some and great impairment of the estates of divers others". A rate being levied, the town bought two substantial engines of brass and their carriages for the purpose, as the phrase went, of "beating and drowning" of fires. Twenty years later, in 1675, the council found it necessary to issue very definite instructions as to how to handle these engines. One would have thought that in the interim sufficient experience would have been gained to make instructions unnecessary. The entry runs:

The Order how the Towne Engine is to be kept. Lett the engine stand halfe full of water at all times, but in ffrosty weather and when a ffrost comes lett out the water and lett it stand empty during the ffrost. Observe when you goe to worke the engine that ffower or ffive men be placed at each end, and lett them lift up their hands with the handles as high as they can and pull downe the handles againe as low as they can and the men to work and make their stroakes jointly and as nere as they can together. The handles are marked, therefore be sure that the handles by putt on at the right side, for there are marks alike on one handle and on one post—viz, two little notches. Lett the pyns be put in their right places againe. There is a wrench to take the engine in pieces, one end thereof unskrewes the inward screwes and another end the other screwes."

There is nothing so effective as explaining in words of one syllable! About this time, one of the minute clerks started using a form of shorthand, and some of his notes have remained on one of the pages containing a list of names.

St. Albans seems to have been fairly well satisfied with Charles II, but in his campaign to obtain absolute power he needed to have control of the House of Commons. Many of the members were chosen by the borough councils, and the king determined to remodel the corporations so that he might have a packed majority in any parliament he might summon. He started by having the corporation of London accused of illegal use of their authority, and when judgment was given against such a powerful body in the King's Bench, its charter was declared forfeited, though the corporation bought it back by agreeing that the king should control the election of the lord mayor, the sheriff and the recorder. By a similar process, or in some cases, by a simple surrender by a terrified corporation, many boroughs lost their charters and had to accept a new one which put power into the hands of the king's friends (now coming to be called Tories), and a Tory majority in the seats of the councils. St. Albans was one of those boroughs. In 1684 the licensee of the Red Lion, a leading local Tory, John Sellioke, was chosen Mayor, and a month later the mayor, aldermen and burgesses yielded up the charter to the king. There is a copy of the document of surrender in the minute book of the council.

At the next parliamentary election Sellioke threatened his fellow-innkeepers with reprisals from the Earl of Marlborough's troops if they did not obey him and vote for the Tory candidate. The king was just dead, and he was succeeded by his brother, James II, and by March 2nd, St. Albans had a new charter. Sellioke continued as mayor, and there were eighteen aldermen instead of the previous ten. But enough Tory citizens could not be found to fill these offices, and some dozen of them were not St. Albans men at all, but gentry from outside. There are only one or two familiar names in the list, one of them being John Gape, and another Edward Seabrooke, of whom more later. We now meet John Churchill, the husband of Sarah Jennings, taking a prominent part for the first time. She was a daughter of the Jennings family of Sandridge and Holywell House, which became her home, so that when she married she brought her husband to live there. Viscount Churchill, which he had

become by this time, was made high steward of the town in
place of Sir Harbottle Grimston. The clerk remained and
was, for the first time, called *Town* Clerk. Some new assistants
were appointed, but they had very little power, most of it
lying in the hands of the mayor and aldermen.

A few months later, in August, even the Mayor was not a
St. Albans man; Henry Guy, of Tring, had been brought in
to fill up one of the posts of alderman, and now he was made
Mayor. He was an absentee Mayor, and his functions were
performed by a deputy with full powers and all privileges.
Needless to say, the deputy was John Sellioke. When, next
year, there were two vacancies among the assistants, the men
who were chosen to fill the places did not turn up to be
installed, and each was fined £10, a very heavy fine, showing
the unpopularity of the post. However, perhaps the size of
the fine made them think twice about keeping up their refusal
to serve, and so the next month they appeared and joined
the council. In September, fifteen non-resident gentlemen
were made freemen for no fee, and these, of course, swelled
the ranks of those who supported the establishment and helped
to send a Tory to parliament. This was a very bad precedent,
and led the way in the next century to a development of
bribery and corruption on a scale not previously seen in the
town.

When the next Mayor was chosen it was Sir Francis Leigh,
also of Tring. One wonders, why Tring? Was there nobody
a few miles nearer who was prepared to back the king?
Moreover, a shortage of Tories in St. Albans strikes one as
somewhat ludicrous today. Like his predecessor he could
not do the work personally, so John Sellioke was appointed
deputy and the stranglehold of the new order continued. But
not for long. The popularity of the king had steadily vanished;
parliament had lost its enthusiasm, and one can perhaps
detect a slightly critical attitude on the part of the council
when, in March 1687, it was ordered that the Mayor should
lay out no money on the repair of the Compter without the
direction of the aldermen. In 1689, after the revolution,
James's charter was annulled, the old charter was restored,
the number of the aldermen was reduced from eighteen to
twelve, and the High Steward, now Earl of Marlborough, had

changed sides and become Whig. As far as records go, never again was a non-local man made Mayor.

Two well-known people were connected with St. Albans during the later seventeenth century. The famous sailor, Admiral Sir Henry Killegrew, acquired property at St. Julian's. After the Dissolution the old hospital was granted to Sir Richard Lee for his brother, and, passing through a number of hands, it came to a London draper, who pulled down the monastic buildings and built a farmhouse. His son sold it in 1693 to Killegrew. After his death in 1712, it again changed hands several times, and eighty or so years later it became the property of the Margrave of Anspach, whose widow sold it in 1820 to a local man. The site of the farm is now built over, and the fine old tithe barn, having become extremely dilapidated, was carefully taken down for eventual re-erection elsewhere. A school off the Watford Road now commemorates the name of Killegrew.

The other celebrity was a member of the local family of Pemberton. Roger, the founder of the almshouses, had a son, Ralph, who became Member of Parliament for the borough and died in 1644, being buried in St. Peter's Church. His son, Francis, became a scholar at the School at the age of six. He took up the law as a profession and was called to the Bar at the age of twenty-nine. He had a brilliant career, and seems to have been created to prove, as the exception, the accusations of the dishonesty of the tribe of lawyers. He was too honest for his time. He rose to the position of sergeant-at-law, and at fifty-four was a judge on the King's Bench. But after one year on the Bench he was dismissed in 1680. He was, however, so outstandingly brilliant that a year later he was chief justice of the King's Bench. Again he was removed to make way for someone of fewer scruples. Still once again he was restored, this time to be chief justice of Common Pleas. He was the judge at the trial of Lord William Russell, of the Rye House Plot, but the powers that be were doubtful if he would agree to the condemnation of another famous defendant in the trial, Algernon Sidney, of whose complicity there were serious doubts, so for the last time Pemberton was removed in favour of the less learned, the atrocious bully, the infamous Judge Jefferies. Pemberton

went back to his practice at the Bar, and was one of the
counsel who defended the Seven Bishops.

James II, in his efforts to make England Catholic once
more, had issued a Declaration of Indulgence, which he
ordered to be read in all churches on a certain Sunday. This
roused great indignation and resistance among both clergy
and laity. "I am bound to read this, but you are not bound
to listen," one clergyman is said to have remarked to his
congregation that day, and waited until the congregation had
risen and left, and then read it to the empty pews. The
Archbishop of Canterbury and six other bishops sent a petition
to the king, praying him not to enforce the reading of the
Declaration, and as a consequence they were arrested and
brought to trial on a charge of libel. Pemberton fought
boldly in his defence of the bishops, and was largely responsible
for obtaining their acquittal in the face of the utmost opposition
by the king and his friends. As a judge his conduct seems to
have been wholly admirable; Chauncy, the Hertfordshire
historian, who knew him, says, "He would not suffer any
lawyers upon tryals before him, to interrupt or banter witnesses
in their evidence, a practice too frequently used by some
counsel in bad causes to stifle truth and obstruct justice, but
allowed every Person liberty to collect his thoughts, and to
speak without fear that the truth might be better discovered."
If we are to consider Dickens reliable in his account of Mr.
Pickwick's trial, Sergeant Buzfuz should have had a few
lessons from Pemberton, C. J., in how to treat witnesses and
defendants. Chauncy goes on, "No temptations of Profit or
Preferment, no Threats, no Menaces of deprivation nor loss of
place nor Honour, could move him to act anything against
the Law". Indeed, a model judge, of whom St. Albans, his
ancestral home, can well be proud.

There is a short description of St. Albans just before 1700
in the travels of Celia Fiennes, the courageous lady, grand-
daughter of Lord Saye and Sele, who travelled all over
England at the turn of the century.

"Thence (from Dunstable) to St. Albans and so we
enter Hartfordshire 12 miles: there is a very large streete
to the Market place, its a pretty towne takeing all, the
St. Juliers and that at one end and the other end is St.

Nicholas, where is a handsome Church; the great Church which is dedicated to St. Albans is much out of repaire; I see the places in the pavement that was worn like holes for kneeling by the devotes of the Religion, and his votery's as they tell you, but the whole Church is so worn away that it mourns for some charitable person to help repaire it; there are severall good houses about the town one" (Holywell House) "of the Earle of Maulberoug and one of Mrs. Gennings" (Jennings) "the Countess Mother".

Her spelling and punctuation are unconventional, and some of her facts are wrong, but we get a picture of the Abbey almost in ruins, and it did not find that charitable person to repair it until the latter part of the nineteenth century, a hundred and seventy years after. The amazing thing is that by the time Lord Grimthorpe started work there was any Abbey to save.

There is another description of St. Albans about this time to be found among the manuscripts of the Duke of Portland. A certain Thomas Baskerville visited the district in his travels in 1671, and he says:

"From Cassabel (Cassiobury) we went to Watford, a market town in Hertfordshire, where the water was then so high, September 24th, 1671, we could not well pass over without wetting our saddles, for which reason we went another way to St. Albans, a great market town about six miles from Watford and about twenty miles from London, in Hertfordshire. St. Albans is a great town with many inns in it, but the Bull Inn is the greatest that I have seen in England. It hath four churches, of these the Abbey Church is biggest, it being an ancient old fabric and now much decayed, but as I heard this year 1681" (? 1671) "they are gathering money by the encouragement of the present Bishop of London. 'Twas built, as they told me, by Offa, King of Mercia, in honour of that saint martyred by the Emperor Diocletian, and in succeeding ages, he had here a rich shrine equivalent to that of Thomas Becket's in the Cathedral of Canterbury. But in the days when popery was turned out of this land, it was taken down and carried to France, as Mrs. Sellioc's son told me, of the 'Lion' where I laid. . . . Here also in this town a great deal of timber is to be bought and sold and gates for highways ready made to be sold."

Was St. Albans a pioneer in prefabrication? "Mrs. Sellioc's son" was John Sellioke, the deputy mayor of later years. In 1700, he or his son of the same name became Mayor in his own right. The Bull Inn stood in Holywell Hill, adjoining the White Hart.

It may seem surprising that in a town where there was a great Abbey Church there was a steady growth of Nonconformism, but looking back on our history it may be remembered that in the later Middle Ages, Lollardy had been prevalent in the town, to the indignation of the abbots, and John Ball had preached here and been tried and executed here. So that there may have been a tradition of Puritanism. But by the time of the Tudors it had been overlaid by the cynicism which accompanied the end of the monastery, and religious enthusiasm was at a low ebb. The end of the Tudor period saw some revival of the reforming spirit.

During the Commonwealth the episcopalian incumbents of the churches were replaced by Puritan clergy, and Congregational meetings were held in the Abbey, where the rector, Nathaniel Partridge, was a well-known divine. After the Restoration he was ejected under the Act of Uniformity, and the Nonconformist movement went underground. For ten years the adherents to its doctrines met furtively at "New House", the home of William Aleward. It is not known where New House was, but it seems unlikely that it was anywhere near the middle of the town, where secrecy would have been difficult. On the other hand, there is a road called New House Park, in the Mile House area, quite near the ancient road from Barnet through Shenley, and it is not impossible that William Aleward lived somewhere about here.

After 1672 the Declaration of Indulgence set the group free from the necessity of secrecy, and it met openly at the house of Robert Pemberton in St. Peter's Street. His family had always been strongly Puritan, even in early Stuart times, and now the house became licensed as a Nonconformist meeting-house. In 1698 the group was strong enough to build a chapel, the Independent Chapel in Lower Dagnall Street. The building still stands, though it has descended from being a house of God to a storage space for a waste-paper merchant!

One of the congregation there was Dr. Philip Doddridge. He had been educated at a private school which had taken over the house of Colonel Alban Cox in Cock Lane (Hatfield Road), afterwards the site of the Marlborough Buildings. His guardian lost all Doddridge's money, and he was befriended by the minister of the Independent Chapel. He became a well-known divine, and is the author of the beautiful hymn, "O God of Bethel". Another member was Dr. Nathaniel Cotton, who carried on a college for the insane in Spicer Street on a site now largely covered by College Street, which was cut when Verulam Road, part of Telford's Holyhead Road, was constructed. One of Cotton's patients for two years was the poet Cowper, whose religious views coincided with his own, and he was visited there by Rev. John Newton, a friend of the poet, when the latter was giving anxiety to his friends owing to his mental condition. The college, which was a pleasant, undistinguished building of the seventeenth century, was partly demolished when the street was cut, but the remains were standing in the early years of this century. It was pulled down later and a shoe factory rose in its place.

To complete the story of the Dissenters in St. Albans in the eighteenth century, some members broke away and found a meeting-place at the Cotton Mill, but later on still they took a building in Long Butt Lane, another name for Shropshire Lane, which was renamed Sweetbriar Lane, and then in Victorian times became Victoria Street. By 1811 the congregation had outgrown this building, and was sufficient to make a proper chapel necessary, so the one was built which still functions in Spicer Street.

Wesley's *Journal* contains four references to visits to St. Albans. In 1748 he passed through on a journey from Derbyshire to London, and in 1759, when going from London to Bedford. In 1771 he tells how he stopped here to see the Abbey, and in 1782, in December, he passed through in an open chaise, which was the only vehicle to be had. He was eighty-two and he developed a bad cough which was difficult to shake off. One must admire the gallant spirit of the indomitable old man bearing such hardship at such a great age to serve his Lord.

CHAPTER THIRTEEN

WHIGS AND TORIES

S<small>T. ALBANS</small>, as a corporate town, sent two members to Parliament, but the number of voters was very small. Even as late as 1831 there were only about six hundred voters on the electoral roll. The right of election was vested in the Mayor, Aldermen and freemen, and the local householders paying scot and lot (a local tax). As the *Victoria County History* says, "For over a hundred years parliamentary representation was in the hands of two families, the Jennings of Holywell House and Water End, with their descendants, the Churchills and the Spencers, on the one hand, and the Grimstons on the other". During the Commonwealth the Gorhambury estates had been acquired in 1652 from the trustees by Sir Harbottle Grimston, a member of an Essex family, who had been a member of the Long Parliament. At first on the side of parliament, his views changed, and he refused to subscribe to the Solemn League and Covenant and left the House. He was one of the commissioners sent to Carisbrooke Castle to try to get some arrangement between the king and parliament, but Charles, obstinate and stupid, lost his last chance, and his death followed inevitably. Harbottle Grimston was considered what in modern jargon is called a deviationist, and went to prison until after the execution. Then released, though still opposed to Cromwell, he continued his legal work and bought Gorhambury for a home nearer to London than his Essex estate. He had married, as his second wife, the widow of Thomas Meautys, Anne Bacon, the daughter of Sir Nathaniel Bacon, the gifted artist, and through her the great collection of Bacon pictures, the glory of Gorhambury, passed to the Grimston family, to be added to the already fine collection of Grimston pictures. At the Restoration, Harbottle Grimston became Master of the Rolls, and his portrait hangs in the Town Hall, St. Albans, on loan from the Earl of Verulam. The history of St. Albans since the Reformation has not been notable for great events, and there have been only a few famous men; our sons have been mainly a respectable but undistinguished company. Sir Harbottle is one of the exceptions, one of the few Albanians who have been nationally distinguished. He was what old St. Albans people called, until quite recently, a "foreigner", but he takes his place between Francis Bacon and Francis Pemberton to bring honour on the town.

John Jennings, son-in-law of Ralph Rowlatt, sat for St. Albans all through the Long Parliament, followed by his son, the father of Sarah, who was christened in the Abbey. When Sarah married John Churchill, as has been said before, she received Holywell House as part of her dower, and she and her husband lived there frequently and loved it. There they were visited by Princess Anne (later queen) and her husband, George of Denmark, of whom Charles II is said to have remarked, "I have tried him drunk and I have tried him sober, and there is nothing in him". George I is said to have visited the Marlboroughs, as they had by that time become. In a letter dated 1714 the Duchess wrote, "However ordinary Holywell House may be, I would not part with it for any house I have seen on my travels". Yet Blenheim was in process of being built at the time.

At the end of the seventeenth century the Grimstons were Whigs and the Jennings Tories, but the parties were not as clear-cut as today, and people were Tories at one period and Whigs at another without being accused of being turncoats. It follows, therefore, that one cannot lay the fault of inconsistency at the doors of either Churchills or Grimstons for the fact that at one election they might be fighting one another, and at the next have formed a coalition and held one seat each.

When in the latter part of the seventeenth century the Churchills were engrossed in court intrigue, the current Jennings lost his seat, and Samuel Grimston, Harbottle's son, became Member. When James II succeeded to the throne, failing to get his Declaration of Indulgence through parliament, he endeavoured to capture the House of Commons, as was related earlier, and St. Albans received a new charter and a new council. The day before the next election, the Mayor started to make new freemen to pack the electorate. He admitted forty-six on whom he could depend, and refused others, even if they were the sons of freemen and could claim admission by right. Churchill and his colleague, Docwra (a very old Hertfordshire name in various forms), were elected, of course. Even in that age the corruption was outstanding, and attention was called to it in the House of Commons, but the members were too enthusiastically loyal to attend to the matter and it remained uncondemned. But the first flush of loyalty soon wore off, and members began to refuse some of King James's demands and parliament was dissolved. In St. Albans, Sellioke's mayoralty came to an end, but we then had the period of "foreign" mayors from Tring. After the Revolution the charter of James was annulled, and we went back to government under the old charter. Churchill had deserted James, and was now in high favour with William of Orange, and was created Earl of Marlborough. He had now become a Whig, so both families were, for a time, on the same side, and the new M.P.s were Grimston and George Churchill.

By 1700, Churchill was again Tory, and George stood with Gape for partner. The Mayor at this time was one of our less scrupulous chief citizens. Corruption went to unheard-of lengths. An outrageous number of freemen were created without the formality of asking leave of the aldermen, the Mayor, Edward Seabrooke, relying on the protection of Churchill. The Churchill family were now at the height of their power, Lady Marlborough being virtual dictator at court through her immense influence over Queen Anne.

But just at this time Churchill went abroad, and Sarah, with a change of heart, threw Seabrooke overboard. He was sued in 1702 and had to face the music. He lost his office, and for several years was being asked to give up the corporation plate. Nowadays, the plate is put out on show on the annual mayor-making day, and a token presentation made to place it in the Mayor's charge for his term of office. Afterwards it goes back in the strong-room and is only occasionally brought out during the next twelve months. But in the eighteenth century the plate really passed into the Mayor's charge, and he took it home and used it. Seabrooke endeavoured to misappropriate it, or so it would seem. On one occasion the Mayor and the town clerk and the sergeant went to his

house and delivered a *mandamus* demanding the return of
the plate. In 1704 other efforts were made in August and
November. The corporation plate was then valued at £30.
All this time Seabrooke was astonishingly left in his office as
alderman, but his intransigence was now too much for the
council, so they turned him out. By 1705 it was obvious that
drastic measures were overdue, and a lawyer was appointed
to conduct a case against him, and he evidently gave in at
last, as no more is heard of the case. Another Mayor, a few
years later, also tried to stick to the plate, and had to be forced
to give it up. St. Albans has not as much corporation plate
as many towns of its age, and one may legitimately wonder if
this sort of thing had happened before, and the misappro-
priators had got away with it. Anyway, why are there a
number of odd spoons and not a set?

In the election of 1705 Sarah, the Duchess, took charge of
the election campaign, but was unable to prevent the return
of Gape, who, however, was unseated afterwards for bribery
and corruption. He, in his turn, got his rival unseated for the
same reason, so neither of the parties in St. Albans could
show righteous indignation at the base tactics of the other
side; they were both tarred with the same brush. It was a
classic case of the pot and the kettle. Sarah had been so
prominent in the election that, in 1710, her husband wrote to
her warning her from coming to St. Albans for the election
of that year for fear of insults. The Mayor had promised his
support to Mr. Lomax, who lived at Childwickbury, but the
Duchess put pressure on him to transfer his support to her
candidates, Mr. Clayton and Mr. Gore. This incident
formed one of the episodes of the millenary pageant of 1948.
A public office of bribery was opened at the town clerk's house,
and standard sums were agreed on. The Mayor carried on
the bad custom of making freemen from outside the town.
Sarah then brought the power of ridicule to bear on the
conflict. Grimston, in his youth, had written a play, "Love
in a Hollow Tree", which was sufficiently bad to be satirised
by both Pope and Swift. He had withdrawn it from sale,
and no doubt hoped that most people had forgotten this early
indiscretion. But Sarah ferreted it out from its obscurity and
reprinted it, with a frontispiece showing a coroneted ass and

an elephant dancing on a tight-rope, which she dedicated to "The Right Sensible the Lord of Flame". The exact point of this elegant wit escapes us nowadays, but it made the candidate a laughing-stock when the Duchess had it distributed among the electors.

By 1727 the cost of bribery had increased to such an extent that the Duchess declared that she wanted to get her grandson elected, but could not do so without spending £1,000 from her own pocket, and so she was going to have nothing more to do with it. However, she did make another attempt two years later, and tried to make a bargain with the Grimstons for young Grimston not to oppose her grandson, Lord Spencer, since they were both standing in the Whig interest. A little glimpse of what an election meant to the local gentry is given in a paragraph in the *London Evening Post* of Saturday, March 24th, 1730:

"Yesterday came on the Election for the Borough of St. Alban's in Hertfordshire, in the Room of Caleb Lomax, Esq., deceased: In the Morning the Lord Viscount Grimston gave a very elegant Breakfast at his Seat of Gorhambury near St. Alban's to Mr. Gape's Friends: after which his Lordship, Sir Tho. Saunders Seabright, Bart., and Charles Caesar, Esq. (the two Knights of the Shire), Francis Goulston, Esq. (the High Sheriff), Humphry Parsons, Esq., Richard Lockwood, Esq., with the principal Gentlemen of the County, rode, attended by about 300 Voters all on Horseback, to St. Alban's in order to Poll, which was continued for about three Hours and a half, and about Four Mr. Brassey flung up the same, when the Numbers stood thus:

> For Thomas Gape, Esq.;   396
> Mr. Brassey;   136

Upon which the former was declared duly Elected: In the Evening the Lord Viscount Grimston gave a Ball to the Ladies, and the Town was illuminated, Bonfires made and such Rejoycings made there as has not been seen for many Yeares: *which shews what Regard is paid to those Gentlemen who are elected with no other view than to serve their Country.*"

The hustings were usually set up near the Clock Tower.

Packing of the electorate continued and reached its climax in 1743, when over a hundred strangers were admitted to freedom. So much indignation was expressed among the general public that this method was abandoned for future elections and straight bribery was used instead.

Towards the end of the eighteenth century the Tories settled down under the leadership of the Grimstons, and the Whigs under the Spencers, the son and grandson of the redoubtable Sarah. In 1796 a man named Waddington spent £5,000 trying to win the seat for the Radicals. He invited the Mayor and a hundred and fifty electors to dinner at the Bull. Every three weeks afterwards free suppers were provided at the same hostelry and at the Red Lion for all electors who chose to take advantage of his generosity. But it was all in vain. The electors ate his dinners and went on voting for somebody else, and discouraged and considerably poorer in pocket he retired from the contest. On one occasion money was being sent from London for the purpose of bribery, but a highwayman intercepted the messenger at London Colney, and the money went into other pockets than those of the electors. Of course, highwaymen infested the roads hereabout at the time, and the Duke of Marlborough himself was held up once at South Mymms and lost five hundred pounds.

After the death of the Duchess of Marlborough the Hertfordshire property passed to her great grandson, Earl Spencer, whose descendants still hold property in the city. His widow lived at Holywell House and was a local benefactor, of whom we shall hear later.

In the election of 1807 bribery was rampant, as usual. One man expected twenty pounds for his vote, but he lost the money because for some reason he did not cast his vote. He considered this a grievance, but Lord Verulam (the Grimstons had by this time acquired a higher title) wrote and said that he hoped he would consider a gratuity of fifteen pounds an ample remuneration for his friendship. Most electors did not get quite such a handsome return, even if they did actually go to the poll, though as each had two votes they often split them and took bribes from both sides. This was recognised by the bribers, and a tariff was established by which a plumper who cast his votes for only one candidate got more than one who split his votes. The Verulam interest continued to return one member up to the date of the 1832 Reform Act.

One of the Members of Parliament for St. Albans in the eighteenth century was James West, who was returned in 1741 with the support of the Grimstons, but violently opposed by the Duchess, now eighty years of age, but still active and forthright in her opinions. One of West's supporters wrote to him,

"I hear . . . the old Duchess told one that since the Mayor and Aldermen still opposed her interest she would find out a way to be even with them before they were aware, and that one Finedon was with her about one hour and her Graceless spoke much to the same purpose and thumpt her cane to the ground in a rage, saying they know not what they did and another said Spencer would certainly come tomorrow night with another gentleman by the Duchess' order to oppose your honour—we all know she never spares money to gratify her childish pleasure to oppose where her heart is set against."

But there was no candidate, after all, from the Marlborough side, and West and his colleague Ashby were returned. When the Duchess died in 1744 her party went over to the support of West. Her grandson, John, died only two years later at the early age of 38. Horace Walpole unkindly ascribes his death to that fact that he "would not be abridged of those invaluable blessings of an English subject, brandy, small beer and tobacco". His son was only twelve, so there were no possible Spencer candidates for the time being, though in 1753 the Duke of Marlborough put forward a companion for West to act as caretaker until his young nephew came of an age suitable to membership of Parliament. About this time, West became Recorder of St. Albans, but when the Duke of Marlborough died in 1758, he was succeeded by West as High Steward of the town, and West gave up the Recordership. A few years later opposition to West was growing in the town, and attempts were made to find opposition candidates. One of these was Mr. Lomax, of Childwick, probably the son of the Lomax mentioned earlier, and he carried his feelings into action, withdrawing his patronage from tradespeople known to be supporters of West. One of these was Mrs. Langford, the landlady of the White Hart, to whom he wrote asking for his account so that he could pay it, "for you dont expect I or my friends will have any further dealings with you. I cannot help mentioning that I think you do two things unnatural. First for a woman to be busy in an election, secondly you know what I mean". A nasty innuendo! West remained Member until the election of 1768, when he decided not to contest the seat again. He had had a pretty bad time for the previous ten years, and probably retired to his new seat for Boroughbridge with relief. He had been member for St. Albans for twenty-seven years, longer than any other member, and he kept in close touch with his constituency by correspondence on the affairs of the town, and he got the mail to come daily to St. Albans in 1759. We might have had a much worse representative at Westminster.

The sad story of bribery and corruption continued into the nineteenth century. At the election of 1831 the poll book records that "five hundred and sixty-six Resident Electors and ninety Non Resident Freemen Electors polled at this election, making in the whole six hundred and fifty-six; exclusive of six whose votes were rejected". Sir F. Vincent obtained 452 votes, Mr. Richard Godson, 422, and Lord Viscount Verulam, 308.

It is fascinating to read the list of voters, so many of the names being represented in St. Albans today or until very recently. Some of them were tradespeople. William Climance was a baker; I used to buy bread at Climance's some fifty years ago. James Dorant was described as gentleman; his descendants were until recently auctioneers and the name was continued by their successor. I can remember little Mr. Dorant, about five foot nothing, always wearing a shiny top hat. Richard Gibbs was a stationer; he founded the *Herts Advertiser and St. Albans Times*, and a nationally known printing firm Gibbs and Bamforth, Ltd., Jesse Hulks was a cordwainer or (shoemaker); another Jesse Hulks made me a pair of boots before the First World War. Thomas Younger was an upholsterer; Younger's still have a furniture business in George Street, though they have added a "do-it-yourself" line. James

F

Deayton was a victualler. It was only between the wars that the name ceased to appear over a grocer's shop in Holywell Hill.

And so one could go on. Despite the growth of the city and the coming of the chain stores, one can still find reminders of the older St. Albans among the shops that still exist, and many more among the memories of the not-so-old inhabitants. Many more of the names of the electors of that time who are not represented among the tradesmen are to be found in the local directory and telephone books. There are several Cherrys, some Gazeleys, a Hester, an Ironmonger, several Kents and Richardsons and Bacons, and other names found then and now include Brackley, Chambers, Crouch, Elborn, Kentish, Lines, Lipscombe, Munt, Pinnock, Steabben, Verney and Westell. Many of these may be, and probably are, descendants of the earlier representatives of their names, and others have only recently vanished from the directory. In fact, scratch a little below the surface of modern St. Albans, with its accents from all over the country, and you will find the genuine St. Albans families, with hundreds of years of history behind them with names like Dockree, scions of the ancient Hertfordshire family of gentlefolk, the Docwras. The Thrales, who run the Water End Barn Restaurant, had an ancestor who made a will in 1542 and lived in Sandridge.

The Act of 1832 gave the right of election to sixty-three freemen, sixty-six inhabitants paying lot and scot, and three hundred and fifty-four "ten-pound householders". Bribery became more expensive but it continued, and the scandal came to a head in 1850, when the corruption was so flagrant that a petition was presented to parliament which set up a parliamentary committee. This unhappily was unable to make a proper enquiry, as it could not summon evidence on subpoena, and some of the principal witnesses absconded. So a parliamentary commission was substituted, which sat from October 1851 to January 1852. It reported that some of the electors had been up to London, hawking the borough about for sale. The cost of elections since 1832 had been over £27,000, of which £24,600 had been spent in bribery. Any-one who wishes to wade in masses of sordid detail can read the report of the Commission, which is in the St. Albans Public Library. Public indignation caused swift action, and as a result St. Albans lost its separate members, and from then on became merely a part of a county constituency, in which corruption was much less widespread. Votes in the countryside were gained not by bribery so much as by intimidation by the landed gentry, and there was not so much opportunity for the St. Albans electors to turn a dishonest penny at election times. What chance they had was finished by the Ballot Act of 1870, for no candidate was going to waste money in bribery when it would be impossible to know if the voter were going to keep his promise and earn his money. Since 1852 successive redistributions have pared off one part after another of the division which included St. Albans, until the removal of Welwyn Garden City and Hatfield, has returned it to almost the pre-1862 position, the only voters outside the city being in the immediate rural area.

CHAPTER FOURTEEN

LIFE IN ST. ALBANS IN THE
EIGHTEENTH CENTURY

A T the beginning of the eighteenth century St. Albans was still a small country town. The two roads from London came, one the Watling Street, through Radlett and Park Street, past St. Stephen's Church, and then up Holywell Hill, as the Saxon abbot had designed so long ago. Holywell Hill was not quite on the line it now has, as the presence of Holywell House pushed the road out to the west, on the line which still exists as a little backwater behind houses near the river bridge. The other road came from Barnet, at first along the old London Road to Sopwell Lane, and then turned north up Holywell Hill, and both turned into the High Street and then down George Street and Fishpool Street and so out of the town. North from the Peahen crossing went Chequer Street, with a big house, an inn, standing out almost in the middle of the road, so that traffic had to go round the east side of it, there being room on the west side for a footpath only. This was the Red House, which continued to obstruct traffic until the beginning of the nineteenth century. St. Peter's Street contained a succession of ponds, one near the church and one where the Market Square is, in front of some cottages, Clark's Almshouses, which were later pulled down to make way for the new town hall, and the charity transferred to some new buildings in Catherine Street. St. Peter's Street was the aristocratic quarter of the town, and most of the prominent people had houses there. The Pembertons occupied the house near the corner of Shropshire Lane, Lady Alicia Jennings lived for a time at the Mansion, and could look out on the Bullring. The Grange, the office of the Chief Executive Officer, was built about the middle of the century by John Osborne, and the grounds form the site of the civic centre. The Kentishes had a house somewhere in the neighbourhood. They were a family with several branches, some of which had gone down and some up. Several of them are buried in St. Peter's Church or St. Stephen's, and according to a writer who did a collection of local sketches with notes about 1797, there were Gentlemen Kentishes, Tradesmen Kentishes, Husbandmen Kentishes and Labourers Kentishes. In the register of wills in the county archives there is a will of two Kentish brothers dated 1574. There was a still earlier Kentish who was a trustee of the Clock Tower in the fifteenth century. In 1711 Thomas Kentish of Sandridge, by his will, set up an elaborate trust for the education and apprenticeship of four boys of the name of Kentish or, failing the name, four boys of his lineage. This trust still continues, and there are still Kentishes in St. Albans and the neighbourhood, though the beneficiaries of the trust may come from great distances, and on occasion the advertisement giving notice of vacancies has been published in Australian papers, since some of the Kentishes are known to have emigrated. The funds are drawn from the proceeds of a farm in Bedfordshire, and the trustees consist of representatives of the St. Albans City Council, London University, the Bedfordshire County Agricultural Committee, and local industrialists and educationists.

With so many coaches passing through the town every day, several of the inns having their own coach service, the turn from Holywell Hill and the narrow George Street and Fishpool Street were an ever-present danger to traffic, and many serious accidents occurred. The surface of the roads was bad, and coaches were turned over in ruts and holes quite close to the town. Towards the end of the eighteenth century the road engineer Thomas Telford was given the task of realigning and reconstructing the Holyhead Road, and in course of time cut a new London Road into St. Albans. This was in 1794. It diverged from the Old London Road near where the railway bridge is now, and the roadmaker had to cut through a hill near the present Alma Road. The bank which was left on either side can still be seen. There was a hollow to the westward and that had to be filled up. Its remains can be seen in the great dip behind the Odeon Cinema. There was a tollgate erected across the new road, where the two roads forked on the site of the present garage, and the flats near it show the height of the bank which was cut through. Soon houses began to appear along the new road, and a few charming Regency houses still exist, though many have been demolished in recent times. Having brought a reasonably convenient road into the town, it was necessary for Telford to make a good outlet in the northern direction, so a new section of the Watling Street was constructed by cutting through the inn-yards of the Red Lion and the Fleur de Lys. This part was cut in 1825 and formed the Verulam Road. It joined on to the old Watling Street just beyond Shafford Bridge, on the way to Redbourn. As the part of Watling Street on the way to Gorhambury was discontinued, the Earl of Verulam enclosed it and made it part of his drive. A few houses were built along the new road, and one of them was the fine building called the Verulam Arms, in which Princess Victoria had lunch with her mother, the Duchess of Kent, on their way to London in 1835, the only time she is known to have visited the town. The house was then a coaching inn, but it never flourished, and when the railway came it failed and became a private house for many years. In the twentieth century it was, for a time, the bishop's palace, but the noise of the constant traffic on the Watling Street was so distracting that Bishop Furse very sensibly moved to the present Abbey Gate House, and Verulam House is now Diocesan House.

Many people are puzzled to see along the Hatfield Road milestones giving the mileage from St. Albans to Reading. One of these is in the forcourt of the City Museum. A road was constructed joining Hatfield and the Bath Road by Lord Cecil in 1700, largely for his convenience. He suffered from gout and wanted a smoother road than the existing track. Later, the Reading and Hatfield Turnpike Trust was set up, and the present Hatfield Road was constructed to take the place of the rough track which continued Cock Lane from the Marlborough Buildings. In its intention to provide a passage across the country avoiding London, it is one of the earliest examples of a by-pass road specifically constructed for the purpose.

In the year 1732 the Duchess of Marlborough acquired by purchase from the family of Rowbotham the manor of Newland Squillers, in the parish of St. Peter. The Manor House stood near the boundary of the town, in Cock Lane, and in this house had lived Col. Alban Cox, friend of Cromwell. Later it had become a school, which had a high reputation among Dissenters as has been said earlier. At this school Dr. Philip Doddridge and Dr. Aitkin, two famous Noncon-formist divines, had received their education, and many Dissenting ministers and professional people had been scholars there. The Duchess had the house pulled down. There is an interesting reference in the *London Evening Post* for February 24th to 26th, 1733:

> "On Saturday several Workmen and other Artificers began to take down divers old buildings at St. Albans by order of her Grace the Dutchess Dowager of Marlborough, in order to raise a noble Building for the relief of 40 poor families of that Town, and her Grace will leave a Sum sufficient to endow it forever; the same is to be carry'd on with the utmost Expedition after a Plan she has already approv'd of."

It is interesting to note that apparently the buildings were intended originally as a housing estate, not an almshouse for old people. The next month the same paper reported that she had set out for St. Albans to look at the new building which had already been begun. Three years later the *Weekly Miscellany* reported that "A statue of her late Majesty Queen Anne is carving out of a Block of white Marble, by Mr. Rysbrach, of Oxford Road, by Order of her Grace the Duchess of Marlborough, in order to be set up in the Court of the New Building which her Grace has lately erected at St. Alban's for the reception of a great number of poor families". As far as can be ascertained, this statue was never set up in the quad-rangle of the Marlborough Buildings, and is, in fact, in the library at Blenheim Palace. In her will the Duchess Sarah left £20 to be paid to the rector of the Abbey Church, or to the vicar of St. Peter's "for overlooking the poor that shall be placed in the said Almshouses". Thus a new charity arose in the town. Education was also largely a matter of charity. The School had sunk to such depths that it was noted about 1800 as being of little public service. In fact it has been stated that between 1750 and 1803 the School was never opened as a public school. The head, usually the Rector of the Abbey, kept a few pupils of his own, not in the Lady Chapel, but in his house, and sometimes in the morning he would take one of his seven or eight scholars, go down to the Lady Chapel, open the door, walk round, walk out and lock up again.

On the other hand, there were several flourishing charity schools. One was founded by the Dowager Countess Spencer for girls in the north-west angle of a field now covered by Thorpe Road, at the end of Belmont Hill. The girls wore a uniform and it was known as the Greencoat School. It remained until her death in 1814. There was another school supported by Viscountess Grimston for the education and clothing of twelve girls. This vanished during the early nineteenth century. A Bluecoat School for boys lasted for many years, having been set up early in the eighteenth century. Thirty-five boys were to be fully clothed, instructed in the principles of the Christian religion according to the rites of the Church of England, and taught to read and write and cast accounts. This was supported entirely by voluntary subscriptions.

The Dissenters played an honourable part in educating the children of St. Albans. A charity school was set up in Dagnall Street in 1712, which clothed and educated thirty boys and ten girls. An Independent Sunday School also clothed and educated twelve boys and eight girls, and educated others without clothing them. There is an interesting document recently discovered in a private house giving the names of many of the children educated in one of the charity schools, though there is a little uncertainty which school. It consists of narrow strips of parchment sewn together, some yards in length, mainly consisting of a list of names, many of which are familiar today, and dating from 1747 to 1780 mainly, though there are some names dated 1740. The scholars included both boys and girls, though there are not many of the latter. It is interesting to look down the list of names, and, as in the list of voters, to recognise names in the modern directory, such names as Dollomore, Bygrave, Lockey, Lines, Puddephatt, Element, Elborn, Weatherley, Souter, Poacock and Crouch. Some are nowadays spelt slightly differently, but they are obviously the same names, and their owners may be descendants of those eighteenth-century little boys and girls who appear to have been admitted at the age of eight years. The

Bluecoat School was maintained in the house of John Hilliard, the vestry clerk, with a roll of twenty-four boys, and his son succeeded him for a short time. It is noted in the council minutes that the Rev. Mr. Preedy acquainted the council that he had no scholars to teach in the School itself, but was ready and willing to teach as many as should be sent him. As it was supposed to be a free school, there should have been no lack of scholars, but the intentions of the authority were being flouted and the Master preferred to teach paying pupils and refused others. The charity schools finally vanished when the Abbey National School was opened in Spicer Street, and later a school board was set up in the town in the second half of the nineteenth century.

There is an enthralling set of Mayor's Account Books. When the Mayor had finished his year of office he submitted an account of what he had necessarily spent and was re-imbursed. For certain items he was allowed a definite amount, but other items were not so specified. He gave a number of official dinners, for which there was a regular allowance. For instance, in 1731 the Mayor's account starts with Michaelmas Day, which was mayor-making day. After the installation and the swearing-in of the new Mayor, he went the rounds with the constables, and tipped them five shillings. He then gave a dinner to the Recorder and various gentlemen, and it cost him one pound ten shillings. During the year he gave five dinners, three of them for quarter sessions.

In the following year the Mayor spent five shillings in drinking the king's health, and asked for a definite amount of twelve pounds to cover his annual expenses. His successor paid the constable and the beadle five shillings for whipping a man, and he spent a pound at the declaration of the poll at the parliamentary election. In 1733 occurs an item for keeping the town clock and ringing the bell: £4, and "Paid the Town Clerk his salary as usual, £2, and for entering orders in the Court Book for one year, £1, and for making and copying this account 5s." In September he paid ten shillings for "ten dozen of Plumb Cakes", and a pound for ten bottles of burnt wine.

Another Mayor claimed for money spent on the constables going the rounds, five shillings and twenty-seven shillings spent at the Red Lion on the constables and the linkmen. The same Mayor paid two pounds for cakes and wine on Michaelmas Day, evidently the refreshments at his reception. It costs a little more nowadays! The next month he paid for drinking the King's health and Admiral Vernon's health, and beer for the sack carriers, whoever they may have been, and he gave an expensive dinner which cost £8.

The following month he twice had to drink the King's health, which one imagines was the equivalent of the modern "Take wine with the Mayor", and was, in fact, a little party. Again we find an entry: "Payed Mr. Rymer for the Liquor for the Constables attending William Bastin to be whipt round the town, 5s. and payed ditto attending John Snedker in the Pillory, 5s."

In 1740 it appears that after Sunday morning service, at which the Mayor was attended by councillors and aldermen by rota, two at a time, he was greeted by the ringing of bells, and he paid £8 for the "Sunday Chimers". There is a full account of the cost of the mayor-making ceremony for this Mayor, 1739–40. "Spend on Constables going rounds, 5s.; Spent that night at the White Hart, £1 12s. 6d.: Paid for certificate of administering the Oath, 2. Paid for cakes and wine, £2. Paid for dinner and wine, £2 10s."

There was a private meeting of some of the council to decide what names to nominate for the next mayor. It was the custom always to put forward two for the council to choose from, and under date January 20th, 1740, we find the entry: "Spent at Red Lyon to settle choice of Mayor, 16s." There is a hint of the beginnings of the highways department in this entry: "Paid to the Scavengers as usual, £1 1s." Probably these were the people who ceremonially (or of necessity) swept the roads before the procession of Mayor and Council, as one of the London Livery Companies still does on ceremonial occasions.

By the next year it is obvious that prices had risen, as the Mayor's feast cost £20, and four guineas was paid to a Mr. John Domville for "dressing this dinner". Perhaps he was a special chef. For a simpler dinner at the Red Lion to celebrate the day of the declaration of peace was paid the sum of £4 2s., and the dinner to the committee choosing the new Mayor had risen in price from the previous sixteen shillings to nineteen.

There is an interesting entry dated December 16th, 1761: "By cash paid expenses at the White Hart on meeting the Aldermen and Officers to proceed to declare war against Spain, 7s. 6d." This calls up a delicious picture of the City Fathers solemnly declaring war between St. Albans and Spain! The next entry carries on the tale: "By cash paid expenses in the Evening drinking success to the war by the direction of the Aldermen: £1 17s." Despite the wording the aldermen did *not* direct the war. In that year the same procedure seems to have been adopted in the choice of alderman as for Mayor, for the last entry for 1761-2 is: "Paid at the White Hart being previous meeting for choice of an alderman, £1." The price had gone up again, or perhaps the White Hart was a little dearer than the Red Lion.

These accounts go on into the nineteenth century, and by then we get such information as that the cost of the sessions dinner had risen to £10 and the Mayor's feast to £15; drinking the king's health four times cost a guinea a time, and the town clerk's salary and bill were lumped together and came to £10 10s. 2d. For the first time we hear of income tax; the corporation paid ten shillings and fourpence income tax in 1800.

The council minutes continue to be enlightening. In 1715 the city loan began. There is an entry, "Two hundred pounds to be borrowed to pay debts owing by the corporation to various people". In 1700 we nearly lost the Clock Tower. The council passed a resolution by eight votes to five that the Clock House should be pulled down and a new Market House built. This resolution was never acted on, and later on Earl Spencer gave the town a Market House, and many were the grumbles in the council as to the mean way in which the corporation had put it up; several said that it was an insult to the generous donor. The minutes of the same year as the vote on the Clock Tower note that the council agreed to allow the payment of a maximum of £5 for the use of cutlery for the mayoral feast, and decided that the number of guests should not exceed two hundred. Where did they find a room big enough to dine such a number? One hundred and twenty years later there arose the same difficulty of the provision of cutlery, and it was decided that kitchen utensils, plates, knives and forks, tablecloths and other necessary items should be purchased for use at corporation dinners, but the aldermen were advised to provide individually at their own expense each two silver forks, a silver tablespoon and silver dessert spoon with the corporation arms engraved thereon.

After the election of 1741 the council meeting was held at the Red Lion, the business being to make the return of the election of West and Ashby. Modern Mayors find the office a full-time job, but at least they do not have to ask leave of the council to take a holiday. There are several entries like this: "Ten days leave of absence was given to the Mayor, August 25th, 1738."

The minutes reflect the corruption involved in admitting freemen in great numbers to influence elections, as related earlier. In 1743 there are a whole series of entries: "Court held May 4th—thirty-five gentlemen admitted free." "Court held May 11th—thirty-nine more gentlemen admitted gratis. Adjourned to the Red Lion." "Court held May 18th— Eight others admitted gratis. Adjourned to the Red Lion." "Court held May 25th—ten persons were admitted gratis. Adjourned to the Red Lion." And so on, weekly, a number of people were made freemen right up to September 7th, and though they did not always adjourn to the Red Lion, sometimes they went to the White Hart, and in one case to the White Horse.

We are told of the price of bread in the market in November 1751. The penny white loaf weighed 8 oz. 7 dr.; the wheaten loaf 12 oz. 10 dr.; and household loaf, 14 oz. 8 dr. There were also twopenny loaves, quarten loaves, half-peck and peck loaves and the last named weighed 17 lb. 6 oz. 1 dr. All loaves had to be stamped with the letters W for white, WH for wheaten, and H for household, together with the first letters of the Christian and surname of the bakers.

There are some suggestions made that the council was suffering from shortage of money, for in January 1740 there is a decision that in future the Mayor should not hold a feast nor buy any provisions or entertainment to be given in lieu thereof. If it were not due to financial stress it is difficult to see why such a slight should have been shown to poor Mr.

Nicoll, the Mayor of the time. But fourteen years later the fact is openly admitted. At the council meeting of September 2nd, 1754, a resolution was passed that because of the debts and expenses of the corporation, instead of attending the Mayor from church to his own house, the aldermen and common council do attend him only at, from and to the town hall, morning and afternoon, on such Sundays as he goes to the Abbey Church. How this was going to save money is not clear. Then the allowances to be made to the Mayor are definitely set down. He was evidently not to be allowed to indulge in a spending orgy during his year of office. The following year the council loan had been added to by borrowing a thousand pounds at four per cent. The next Mayor had an embarrassing gift. A "buck extraordinary" was presented to the council, and that caused the mayoral feast to exceed the sum allowed by £7 11s., and that had to be debated by the council before the Mayor was "whitewashed" and the extra amount was allowed. The next month the Mayor and a judge were asked to "wait upon Lord and Lady Cowper and desire their interest with the Hon. John Spencer to advance the Corporation such money as they shall think proper towards the discharge of the debts of the Corporation". A week's leave of absence was granted to the mayor for the purpose. Truly the Corporation were in a sorry financial state for them to have to go cap in hand to Mr. Spencer to borrow money. They got £1,000, and the next year they added £250 to their debt to him.

We have only once tried to make a foreign-born inhabitant Mayor, but that happened in 1762. A certain Mr. Vandermeulen had built a house in Romeland, now occupied by the offices of Messrs. Miskin, and he was evidently well liked, for he was invited to become Mayor, but when he was called on to take the oath he refused to do so, for, as he was an unnaturalised alien, he was advised by counsel that he was ineligible. Some years later his son was elected to the office his father could not hold. The father had a daughter, who ran away with the organist of the Abbey, who later committed suicide in School Lane.

Mr. Mayor is not often a man of high scholarship; indeed, in 1617 we had a mayor who could not read or write, and made his mark when he was supposed to sign the roll. But we have at times had learned men on the council. In 1763 Mr. Alderman Parker was given permission to have access to the archives to compare several translations of the charters with the originals. When he had decided which was most accurate a correct translation was to be chained to the bookcase in the Town Hall for the use of the Mayor, Aldermen, Recorder and Town Clerk. This translation does not seem to be in existence. Perhaps it was worn out by use by the less learned members who could not read the originals.

We have heard a good deal about the new idea of pedestrian precincts in shopping areas. Our ancestors in St. Albans were acquainted with the problem and found the same solution, for an entry dated July 1st, 1772, says that the sergeant-at-mace was to call on the occupiers of houses in the Back Market, or Women's Market (i.e. French Row), from the house in the occupation of Jonathan Heylin to the Fleur-de-lys, to acquaint them that it was intended to erect a rail or bar, to be used only on Saturdays, to keep waggons and other carriages from passing through the market.

About this time, the council was faced with expense on account of the Town Hall, which was reported as being ruinous. The matter was referred to a committee, but we do not hear of anything being done for two or three years. Then we are given an estimate from a builder for taking down the kitchen and rebuilding from the foundations. That was to cost £61 2s. 3d. and the money appears to have been found by the sale of two properties, "The Hare" and "The King's Arms", both being reported to be in a ruinous condition. The Hare faced the pillory, in other words, somewhere opposite where Timothy White's shop is, and The King's Arms was next door, by one of the passages still leading through to Chequer Street. The two properties together brought in £80 when sold, which would pay for the repairs at the Town Hall, and the council felt encouraged to beautify it, for early next year they decided to have the chamber wainscotted chair-high and papered above, the beams to be cased, a Portland stone fireplace to be put in, and windows of the "Venetian order" to be put in to make the chamber match with the rest of the Town Hall.

In 1769 we have the unusual spectacle of a woman, Mary

Bowley, being the official keeper of the gaol. Is this the first instance of the St. Albans women in posts of responsibility for which the city is noted today? She held office for ten years, and must be presumed to have been satisfactory and efficient at her job. She was succeeded by a man who was anything but satisfactory, for he acted also as sergeant-at-mace, and he claimed £3 15s. for taking a prisoner to London. The council were outraged at such a charge, and paid him a total of two guineas, and three months later he was given the sack. They would have found it better to have appointed another woman!

An instance of long survival as tradespeople in St. Albans starts in 1794, when the Clock Tower was leased to Thomas Wilkins. In the voters' list of 1831 Edward Wilkins appears as cordwainer or shoemaker, and in the early years of the twentieth century his descendant occupied the old police station in Chequer Street as a saddler. When the station was leased to Donald Black as a children's outfitters, Wilkins' shop moved to St. Peter's Street, still working with leather. This shop closed down between the wars, and the name at last vanished from our streets.

Just before the end of the century there is evidence that cranks are not the product of one age, for some inhabitants of the town petitioned the House of Lords that the new East India Company's charter should contain a clause that facilities "to those benevolent persons desirous of going to India to improve the moral degradation of the immense population . . . shall be given". (Herts County Records.) The names of the signatories include Sam Gutteridge, Thomas Baker and Benjamin Younger.

CHAPTER FIFTEEN

ST. ALBANS IN THE EARLY
NINETEENTH CENTURY

URING the early years of the nineteenth century St. Albans existed in more or less placid obscurity, save for the connection with the wider world occasioned by the passage of the many coaches through the town. Almost the only liveliness must have been found in the numerous inns, where strangers staying for a meal or for the night met the local tradesmen and yokels. Other interests were largely absent, save those of parish-pump politics. We were not much touched by the French wars, though we had a semaphore put on the top of the Clock Tower, a structure which can be seen in old prints. This was erected in 1804, and used as a link in the Dover to Liverpool signal system until dismantled in 1814. But it was used to send the news of the Battle of Trafalgar, and it is recorded that it could send a message to Yarmouth and receive an answer in five minutes, which compares quite favourably with the modern telephone. It was, however, taken down before Waterloo.

We get a picture of St. Albans in 1813 in a curious little book written and published by Solomon George Shaw, a stationer, bookseller and binder in the Market Place. For several reasons Mr. Shaw was very critical of the town, and particularly of its government. He waged a personal vendetta, in words at least, with the corporation. He would appear to have been a councillor who wanted to be an alderman, but was not appointed, and so has nothing good to say about those who failed to recognise his outstanding qualifications for that honour. He remarks sarcastically, "Many of the Assistants" (i.e. councillors) "are, in their private character as respectable as some of the Aldermen" (only some?) "but as public members of the Corporation they must stand aloof. . . . As to the requiring of their assistance and counsel, with the above exceptions" (he lists them) "which is little better than calling them out of respectability to be ridiculed in public, where is no such honour conferred. Whether a jealousy arises on the part of the Aldermen lest the Assistant should promote the public good of the borough more than they, and which would not be very difficult, or from what other cause cannot be ascertained, but a haughty distance is in general observed."

He describes St. Albans' streets in no complimentary terms. He speaks of little lanes and passages, some of them but little calculated to reflect much credit upon those whose duty it was to keep them neat and clean. "That part of the town in which the market place is situated is very confined and from thence to the bottom of St. Peter's Street are several very mean impoverished houses, with all the concomitants of poverty, filth and its nuisances, which a little public spirit would effect the removal of; and thereby render that part of the town much more healthy and respectable." As he lived in the Market Place, he should know!

He liked St. Peter's Street. "St. Peter's Street is a very fine open situation and the most genteel part of the town. . . . There are a few houses which bear marks of great antiquity but the greater part of them have of late been considerably modernised. At a house of Mr. Richard Mason, in High Street, are some carved figures which support the overhanging part of the first storey and are in excellent preservation." That house, which had become a shop, was pulled down between the two World Wars, and the site now houses a grocer's, a wireless shop and others, in a modern building. The carvings were on the side facing Waxhouse Gate Lane and upheld the upper storey, as Shaw described. The house had stood upon the site of the Waxhouse Gate, a large structure of probably three storeys, which was still standing in the eighteenth century, but was then pulled down, possibly by this Mr. Mason.

We seem to have lost track of some ancient glass, for Shaw tells us, "In the windows of the Town Hall there are some specimens of ancient painted glass; there are also two excellent specimens of this art in the house of Mr. Alderman Brown in the High Street, and others at the George Inn; at the Fleur-de-lis Inn is a fine specimen exhibiting the Keys of St. Peter, and others in various parts of the town".

We speak bitterly of the amount of traffic which passes through St. Albans. In their way, our predecessors knew about this. Listen to Shaw: "The mails and stage coaches which run through the town (supposing them to be pretty well loaded) have accommodation for upwards of six hundred passengers daily; add to which the number of travellers which pass through by other conveyances and those on foot, it may reasonably be computed that not less than 1,000 persons pass through the town every day." The noise must have been appalling. The roads were at best cobbled, at worst unmetalled in any way and quagmires in bad weather, while in dry weather they were deeply rutted and incredibly dusty. The coaches had iron-shod wheels, and only the best coaches and the private vehicles were well sprung. Travellers must have been a hardy lot in the beginning of the nineteenth century.

Shaw goes on: "Prior to the improvement of the public roads in England, innumerable quantities of pack-horses were constantly passing through St. Albans with the produce of the factories of Manchester, Nottingham, Stafford, Coventry, etc., and at which period the inns were more numerous than at present; and several large, commodious buildings situated on the roadside (now used for other purposes) can be traced to have afforded accommodation for the weary pack-horse and his driver. There are here cotton and silk mills which give employment to 500 persons, mostly children." The silk mills were established in 1804; we do not know much about the cotton mill, but one of the principal trades for women was straw plaiting, which was a cottage industry. Women could earn five shillings a day, which was a very high wage. There were plait-schools for children, and they were soon sufficiently expert to earn fourteen shillings a week. The plait was sold in School Lane. Later in the nineteenth century straw hat making started, the women taking home great bundles of straw plait and making it into hats on their special machines, then taking it to the many factories which existed in the town, where the blocking became a man's trade, after which the hats were trimmed and finished by women working in the factories. The other main trade in the town was printing, which had survived from the later Middle Ages.

Shaw says that the upper part of the town was poorly

supplied with water, and that it was supplied at a dear rate. Even to this day the city is divided into four zones of water-pressure because it stands so high. One climbs a hill into St. Albans from every direction. In Shaw's time, most families were served from the pump near the Clock Tower, which was erected by the Spencer family, who kept it up for years, "since when, the inhabitants for want of a better sense of independence, lay the burthen of this expense upon the purses of their representatives". (Does one detect a slightly sour note here?) "There is another public pump at the bottom of St. Peter's Street, called the Blue Pump, seldom in repair, therefore of very little service."

The town was organised, as it had been in Elizabethan days, into three wards, Middle Ward, Holywell Ward, and St. Peter's Ward, each with its own constable, appointed at the Court Leet annually. By this time the inhabitants had been given, by Act of Parliament, the right to pave and light the town, and cleanse and regulate the streets; a watch could be kept, but as the watchmen were usually old men who took care to be absent when trouble threatened, one can only imagine what our modern hooligans would have made of them. The bright lads of St. Albans were probably not so different in those days, so the poor old boys' lot was not a happy one.

Both Celia Fiennes and Baskerville described the Abbey as being in very bad repair in the late seventeenth century. Very little seems to have been done to alter this state of affairs by the early nineteenth century, for Shaw tells us that there was not enough room for all the would-be worshippers in the Abbey, because only part of the building was now fitted up for public worship. That was under the tower, with a small part reserved for the boys of the Bluecoat School in the south transept, and two large pews for the corporation, so badly placed as to put the Mayor and the aldermen sitting with their backs to the preacher. Other pews were locked up by the holders, who seldom used them, so the seats available to the general public were very limited. Obviously the nave was in too bad a state to be used for worship, and the Lady Chapel was, of course, in the occupation of the school, and fitted up with forms and other educational paraphernalia.

He gives us some information about the buildings of the town at the time of Waterloo. First, the Town Hall. Here quarter sessions were held. There were two lots of quarter sessions, one for the Liberty (corresponding to the present county division, in the days before the setting up of the county councils), the other for the borough. Other meetings of the corporation were held here also, and in the winter the big room upstairs was used for balls and assemblies. This room was a very long room which could be, at need, divided into separate rooms by partitions. The lower part was still occupied by a gaol, with apartments for the jailer, and the fire-engine was kept there.

He is very caustic at the expense of the Market House. He says that it was built by the corporation, but Lord Spencer offered to pay for it, while allowing the inhabitants to build it to their own taste. He comments "the present humble structure evinces a rigid regard for economy, which certainly ought not to be lost sight of, yet it intimates so low an opinion of his Lordship's intention, which no doubt was to have raised a public building that would have borne a respectable appearance. . . . It is much to be regretted the projectors had not raised a handsome edifice more worthy of so generous a contributor to the public good". It appears that his lordship also was disappointed at the structure that had been put up, for he refused to allow his coat-of-arms to be placed where it had been intended, in the centre of the roof fronting the road. Instead, a figure of Justice was put on the top of the building, a figure which had been removed from the Market Cross, a building over a pump in front of the Clock Tower. Recently a waggon had come into collision with it, and being stronger than the building, the damage was so great that it had to be taken down, and Justice found another home somewhat safer. At least she wasn't going to be charged by mad waggons on the roof of the Market House. The Eleanor Cross had vanished during the eighteenth century; first the top was taken off, and then the rest was removed to make way for the ill-fated Market Cross.

There were apparently three places to which offenders could be sent. One was the gaol in the Great Gateway, known as the Gatehouse. It was said to have several cells and a spacious and airy courtyard for the use of the prisoners during the day. Where this courtyard was is doubtful, but may have been where the headmaster's garden is now. The prisoners were allowed a pound and a half of bread a day, which had been increased from one pound by the Mayor, William Trelss, in 1812. No firing was provided. Passing strangers often heard a pleading voice from within begging them to put alms into an old shoe, which the prisoners let down by string from a window, to enable them to have a fire. On the other side of the road, where the Abbey guesthouse had been, was the house of correction, which occupied part of the building otherwise used as an inn. To this place were usually committed vagrants until they were returned to their respective parishes. Our predecessors were not hospitable to the wayfarers, and had no intention of taking on responsibility for their sustenance. They were sent back whence they came as quickly as possible, even when they were pregnant women. In this they compared poorly with the monks, who allowed, as remarked earlier, a stranger to remain three days, and fed and housed him before they asked awkward questions. Farther away was the Compter, which was under the Town Hall and usually housed petty local offenders.

Cock Lane was beginning to be built on. Shaw notes that there were three houses there, built in 1781 by a goldsmith of London, John Masterman, in lieu of three old ones which stood opposite the White Horse, which he had acquired.

Shaw evidently knew nothing of the history of the school, prior to the reign of Edward VI, whom he regarded as the founder, but he says caustically that "the school at present is generally considered to be of little service". In this comment he was fully justified, but he speaks appreciatively of the charity schools, especially of those set up by Dissenting bodies.

St. Albans must have been a rather dull place to live in at that time, for Shaw tells us that it had no public place of entertainment whatever. In this he was a little unfair, for according to an early playbill there was a performance of "The Dramatist" given at the Theatre, St. Albans, on November 5th, 1792, though where the theatre was is not stated. Probably the performance was given by a troupe of strolling players, such as Nicholas Nickleby joined as juvenile

lead.   Certainly within a very few years of Shaw's strictures
the town was regularly visited by such companies, and it is
stated that they used buildings around the middle of the town,
including the Market House, the Moot Hall, after the building
of the present Town Hall, and the Corn Exchange after that
had been built.   In an extremely interesting article by R. P.
Mander in the *Hertfordshire Countryside Magazine*, 1955, he says
that plays were performed in the early nineteenth century at
the Turf Hotel in Chequer Street, and that there was a travelling theatre which used to visit the town at fair time, and
perform on the Cock Meadow, opposite the Cock in Hatfield
Road.   He tells the story of how, once, when the company
was playing in the town, a fire broke out at the Fleur-de-lys,
and that the actors helped to fight the fire, and Richardson,
their manager, generously donated a hundred pounds towards
the relief of the sufferers.   In return the council gave him the
right to play in the town, not only on fair day but for three
days after.

There was also occasional real excitement, despite what
Shaw says.   *The Star* of May 30th, 1810, reported.

"The town of St. Albans has been the scene of serious
tumult during the last five days.   Several privates of the
local militia, now assembled there, it appears made an
extraordinary demand of about fourteen shillings per man,
which was refused by the officers, in consequence a sergeant
was deputed by the regiment to represent their grievances
to the Commander, which he did in such a way as to give
great offence;   in consequence he was arrested and thrown
into the town jail.   On Sunday afternoon, between 2 and
300 of the militia assembled in front of the prison and
after committing many outrages, they broke open the door
with pikes, etc., and rescued the prisoner.   The officers
assembled as soon as possible, called all the men that
would stand by them, with other forces, and repairing to
the scene of disorder before the jail, they succeeded in
taking into custody 19 of the rioters, without much mischief
occurring.   On Monday, the most refractory of them were
taken from the other jail in the town where they had been
confined all night, and tried before a Court martial.   The
result was that five of the ringleaders were sentenced to

receive a hundred lashes each, and one was ordered 150; these sentences were put into execution. The tumult is not entirely subsided. The officers were threatened with violence, and tumultuous meetings still take place. The magistrates with a strong force, are, however, on the alert, and tranquillity will speedily be restored."

Had Mr. Shaw been writing two years later than he did, he would have had a most important matter to discuss. On February 12th, 1817, the corporation gave leave to bring an intended railway, to Romeland if necessary. We may well be thankful that it was *not* found necessary. It is said that, later on, a suggestion was made that the railway station should be at St. Michael's, but that leave was refused by the Earl of Verulam. If this is so, then blessings on his head! Mercifully, there was no power of compulsory purchase then. Actually the first railway did not come to St. Albans until 1858, and then it was only the branch line from Watford, with the station at the foot of Holywell Hill. The branch to the Great Northern at Hatfield came next, and finally we found ourselves on a main line, the Midland Railway, and a number of innkeepers went bankrupt.

In 1810 there was something of a scandal in the town, for the Recorder was sacked for neglecting his duties. There had been some dispute with him over the appointment of his deputy. He had nominated someone, but the council passed a resolution of disapproval. This was in March. In May the gentleman nominated wrote to the council giving them the information, but they replied by sending him a copy of the resolution, and in June the council decided to take counsel's opinion. The case was heard in the King's Bench in July, and the decision went againt the Recorder's power to nominate. So in November the council decided to get rid of the Recorder, and he went.

In 1814, occurred an event which went some way to justify Shaw's complaint that the councillors were ignored and that all the honours went to the aldermen. An invitation was received by the Mayor, Aldermen, High Steward, Recorder and Town Clerk, but not the councillors, to dine with the Marquis of Salisbury at Hatfield House to meet the Duke of Wellington. Of course they accepted, and decided to take the opportunity

of presenting the freedom of the borough to the Duke, and
the Mayor was commissioned to obtain a gold casket to hold
the scroll. He was authorised to pay fifty guineas. Oddly
enough, the presentation was to be made not by the Mayor,
the obvious person, but by the Recorder, though the Mayor
and aldermen were to appear in their robes. To get the
casket and scroll ready must have been a rush job, for the
order was authorised only on July 15th, and the dinner was
fixed for the 24th.

One of Shaw's complaints was that one of the pumps was
permanently out of order. That was in 1814; in 1817 the
council got round to recognising the fact, and very generously
they gave permission for it to be put in repair by public
subscription. But nobody hurried; it was a leisurely age.
Four years later there is an entry that it was to be repaired by
public subscription. If this was the Blue Pump in St. Peter's
Street it needed it badly, for in 1820 it had been reported
that one, John Peele, was to be prosecuted for stealing the
pipes, etc., of the pump. Within a few years it was destined
to be pulled down to make room for the new Town Hall.
By this time Shaw seems to have left the town, as he is not
on the voters' list of 1821, and was stated to be living in
Hertford, and the earliest local newspaper printed in the
county was printed at Hertford by S. G. Shaw.

In 1822, St. Albans was prepared to take the exciting
step of having gas mains laid. Permission was given to Joseph
Hedley to break up the roads for the purpose, but two years
later he had done nothing, and correspondence took place
with the General Gas Company, which eventually brought gas
to the borough in 1824. Water mains came in 1833, but we
had to wait until 1880 for the beginnings of sewage, and to
cover the town took a good many years.

As the suggestion of a railway in 1817 had come to nothing,
the coach service went on, and in 1826 there were seventy-two
coaches a day passing through. But the St. Albans people
had seen a terrifying sight about that time. Steam engines
for road traffic had been invented in France in the eighteenth
century, and one was developed by William Murdoch, a
pioneer in gas lighting. By the turn of the century experiments
were being carried out by Richard Trevithick. He built a

steam road-engine with a passenger body and a steering-wheel at the front. This, while shown at an exhibition, was not fully developed, but other engineers tried to form companies to exploit the idea, and one of these was the London and St. Albans Steam Carriage Company, and this actually provided a regular service between St. Albans and London via London Colney and Barnet. Such machines were not popular with the turnpike authorities, fearing excessive wear and tear on the roads. By 1835 there were quite a number of these coaches on the roads, some carrying up to fifty passengers at a time. Although a select committee reported that there was no excessive wear, the vested interests induced parliament to tax these useful vehicles out of existence. By doing so they cut off their own noses, for when the railways came and turnpikes and inns alike were ruined, steam engines might have saved something for them out of the wreckage. As it was, only the traction engines of one's remote childhood were left, the Invicta steamrollers and the like, with the red-flag man well in evidence.

There is a survey of St. Peter's parish among the city archives dated 1826. Unfortunately the map which should accompany it is missing, but it gives the early name of the house now mistakenly called Bleak House. In 1826 it was called Folly House, and was in the occupation of one, Samuel Jones, the property including Upper Gumbards, which apparently is the part of Catherine Street between Dalton Street and Church Street, and part of Lower Gumbards, probably the part between Dalton Street and Normandy Road, then a narrow lane. The spelling of the name has changed through the sixteenth century—Gumbedes via Gumbards to the modern Gombards. It also included the meadow on the other side of the road, which was only built over about the beginning of the twentieth century. But by 1832 the house was known as the Daltons. This name seems to connect it with Francis Dalton, who was a county justice in 1719. In 1832 there were eighteen voters in Daltons and the rest of Catherine Street, which is a fairly high number considering the total number of the electorate. Victoria Street had two voters only, but there were eleven in Verulam Road and twelve in New London Road, showing that these roads

were already being built up. There is a most interesting map of
the central part of the town, dated 1827, showing the line of
the new Verulam Road, not yet named but called the New
Road, and College Street, called the New Street. From it
one can trace the further course of the passage called today
Gombards Alley. It appears as a footpath on the east side
of the Gumbards field, and before the cutting of the road it
continued straight on along the eastern boundary of land
belonging to the Rev. John Kentish, to Lower Dagnall Street,
coming out just below the houses now standing on the high
pavement, and again continuing, but apparently not as a
public path, to the house of Mr. Shrubbs in George Street,
near the corner of Spicer Street. The New Street cut off the
wings of the College, which is shown as a long house with
forward-projecting wings on north and south, the greater
part of the wings is shaded as covered by the road. In my
childhood the house had the remains of the wings projecting
only a few feet, and gabled. It seemed small for the purpose
of a private mental home, but this map explains the difficulty.
The whole of the area, now Russell Avenue, and the adjoining
roads, is shown as Kentish property. The Kentishes were local
brewers, and owned a lot of property all over the borough.

The inhabitants of St. Albans at this time must have felt
rather as we do today, when so many familiar landmarks are
disappearing. They saw the New London Road cut and the
Verulam Road, and also in 1837 Holywell House was demolished in order to straighten Holywell Hill, and make it the
road we know. The Red House was taken down in Chequer
Street, giving it a straight passage for traffic, and a new
Town Hall was built.

There had been a lot of discussion about its site when it
was proposed. Two positions were suggested, one the present
site, the other in Romeland. The justices, in 1827, proposed
the Romeland site, but the corporation preferred the St.
Peter's Street position. Although they were notified of this
preference, the justices persisted, and later in the same year
they again asked the council to sell them the Romeland site
for the court house, but the council unanimously refused to
sell at all. Next year the council agreed to co-operate with
the justices and have a combined Town Hall and Court House,

in St. Peter's Street, on condition that the freehold was vested in the corporation. In the end, after lengthy negotiations, the building was vested one-third in the corporation and two-thirds in the magistrates. When in the later nineteenth century the county council was set up, it took over the building, with certain rights reserved to the corporation. The old town hall was sold, and from the erection of the new town hall in 1831, from the plans of George Smith, which can be seen in the County Record Office, the anomaly existed of a corporate body not owning its own town hall. The building is not even properly called town hall, but Court House. With the building of a new court house and a new town hall in the civic centre, the old court house will find some new uses.

From time to time, even in the nineteenth century, the Mayor, with other officials, has perambulated the boundaries, and there is an amusing story told of the 1830 perambulation. The macebearer was attending on the Mayor when he was for some reason attacked and assaulted by two brothers, Joseph and George Taylor. In the fracas that ensued the mace was taken from him and injured. Even as late as 1960 the damage could be seen, one of the arms of the crown being broken. It had, one may add, been very badly mended, with lead solder—an outrage on a beautiful silver-gilt mace of the time of Charles II. It was mended in 1960 properly, and now all trace of the injury has gone. The justly angry Mayor ordered that proceedings should be taken against the offenders, but a few months later the two men concerned attended a council meeting and apologised, and the matter was allowed to drop. What caused the incident is unknown, but the mace in its origin is a weapon, and maybe the macebearer was annoyed by some remark and threatened the brothers with offensive action. Or perhaps they were merely drunk!

Traffic problems existed even then, although the new roads had been cut, and in 1833, the clerk to the Commissioners of Paving and Lighting wrote to the council asking for the removal of the pig-pens erected in the top portion of Dagnall Street on market days, as there was not enough room for traffic, and carts had to drive up on the pavement to get by. We have heard of this nowadays, but not for pig-pens. The

matter was referred to the mayor as clerk of the market, and
no doubt he arranged for the pigs to grunt in another position.
Looking at Dagnall Street, it seems remarkable that the pens
were ever put there.

In the transactions of the St. Albans Architectural and
Archaeological Society for 1929 there is a fascinating article
on St. Albans in the early nineteenth century by Mr. Stanley
Kent, who died in 1961, drawn from his memories of what
his grandfather told him. Born in St. Albans in 1804, the
old gentleman lived until 1900, and between them grandfather
and grandson spanned a period of nearly one hundred and
sixty years of St. Albans history. He tells how, in 1836, a
coach stuck fast in a snowdrift twenty feet deep just where
the railway bridge now crosses London Road, and how, about
the same time, the Holyhead Mail and the Chester Mail had
a race near the same spot, and one trying to pass the other,
a collision occurred in which a passenger lost his life and others
were injured. He says his grandfather remembered when
there were only about half-a-dozen houses between the
Peahen and London Colney.

St. Albans can claim that steeplechasing started in the
neighbourhood. The father of the Grand National may be
said to be Thomas Coleman, who first organised race meetings
here. He began with a race on Nomansland in which George
IV ran a horse, and won the Gorhambury Stakes. Originally
a stable-boy, Coleman had become well known as a trainer,
and he and a jockey friend set up a training establishment
near Wheathampstead, and used the park of Brockett Hall
for gallops. In 1811, Lord Verulam allowed him to train his
horses in Gorhambury Park, and later a racecourse was laid
out in the park. He also took over the management of the
Chequers Inn, and changed its name to the Turf Hotel. It
is now the Queen's Hotel, though only the part south of the
archway which led to the innyard is still licensed; the rest
is a shop. After the successful race in Nomansland the races
were run at Gorhambury, and in 1830 originated the first
regular steeplechase run in England. Local steeplechases
lasted until 1839.

Mr. Kent reminds us of some old buildings in St. Albans
in the early part of the century. He says that the one old

house in Victoria Street, with a lead guttering dated in the eighteenth century, was the Grange Farm then. The Grange itself, built by John Osborne about the middle of the eighteenth century, is still standing, and is the office of the Chief Executive Officer, and is preserved as a feature in the civic centre. The office of Messrs. Rumball and Edwards on St. Peter's Green was the old St. Peter's parish workhouse. Mr. Kent tells of a charitable lady, Miss Cotton, who lived at the Georgian house, opposite St. Peter's Church, and who was so kindly to the poor that she paid them to dig a huge hole in her garden in the winter, and paid them to fill it up again the next winter. Another curious bit of information he gives us is that the famous cedar tree in the Sumpter Yard was planted by the Dowager Countess Spencer on March 25th, 1803, and that the umbrella shape is due to the top being broken off by boys when it was young. So hooligans damaged property even in 1803.

William Cobbett passed through St. Albans on his journeys in 1822. He says that the hay crops were cut by local labour, but the stacks were made by perambulating Irish labourers. He saw the finest ash trees of his life between Redbourn and Hemel Hempstead. He says that the labourers earned between eight and twelve shillings a week. The mowers got two shillings a day and two quarts of strong beer, and as much small beer as they could drink. There was no coffee or tea for them, but a roasted rye drink made from powder at three-farthings a pound. It would appear that "instant" drinks are older than we think. He approved of the husbandry of this part of Hertfordshire, "I did not see three acres of potatoes in the whole tract of the country from St. Albans to Redbourn, and from Harpenden to Chesham". He hated potatoes and never ate them.

The St. Albans people were not entirely deprived of intellectual amusements in those early days of the nineteenth century. In 1823 was set up the St. Albans Literary Society. During the first year, some subjects were studied, according to the official report, which would hardly appeal to the audiences of today; for example—"On the Ravages of Time"; "On Female Heroism"; "On the Public Spirit of the Roman and British People"; "On the Love of Life"; and "On Contentment". These could not be said to be wildly exciting. But they also held debates, and some of these were remarkably advanced in thought. One is startled to find that one of the subjects debated was, "Are the mental powers of the sexes equal?". No doubt the affirmative was defeated, but it is remarkable that it should even have been debated. Another debate was held on the desirability of unlimited freedom of the Press. Particularly modern was the debate on "The Death Penalty for non-violent Crimes".

CHAPTER SIXTEEN

FROM 1835 TO THE END OF THE NINETEENTH CENTURY

IN 1835 the Municipal Reform Act was passed and affected St. Albans along with all other boroughs. No longer were vacancies to be filled by the existing council. Now there were to be elections, and the aldermen were not to sit for life, but be subject to the rule that still obtains, that half the number of aldermen should retire every three years, with one-third of the councillors retiring every year. In St. Albans there were to be four aldermen and twelve councillors for the four wards. There was to be no longer a high steward or a recorder, and the latter had to be compensated for the loss of his office. There was a change, too, in the Abbey. Up to now the advowson had been in the hands of the corporation, and they chose the rector. The new law forbade that a council should own an advowson, so it was sold to the incumbent, the Rev. Dr. Nicholson. Forty years later, when the diocese of St. Albans was created, the advowson passed to the bishop.

At the first election all twelve councillors had to be elected. There had not been much increase in the electorate, and the candidate at the top of the poll received only three hundred and eighteen votes, and the lowest had two hundred and twenty-five. There had been a long list of nominations, thirty of them, giving voters an embarrassment of riches in the way of choice. There was a well-fought fight on strictly party lines. Those who accuse modern politicians of introducing party politics into local elections are ignorant of the history of their own boroughs. The only Liberal to be elected here in 1835 was Richard Webster, and he headed the poll, but the rest of the councillors and all the aldermen were Conservatives. The representatives of the majority party held a victory dinner at the Turf Hotel, which had been their headquarters, and a local band marched round the streets.

The first Mayor under the new Act was John Thomas

Lipscombe, a member of a family which supplied medical men to the town and more than one Mayor, Dr. E. H. Lipscombe holding that office in 1909, seventy-three years later. The next year the Liberals did not contest the election; they tried again in 1837 unsuccessfully, but so vigorously that the *County Press* accused them of bribery. The new council was not very patriotic, rather strangely, in view of their "true blue" complexion. Although in 1837 they presented an address to the queen on her accession, yet the very next year they decided not to recommend any public celebrations of her coronation. But they changed their minds in 1840, and sent an address on the occasion of her marriage. Addresses, of course, cost very little, while public celebrations could cost quite a lot!

As has been said before, in previous times people were not anxious to be councillors. This objection still occasionally occurred, though councillors did not now go so far as cutting up their gowns. In 1838 Mr. Webster, the very man who had been top of the poll in 1835, was fined £25 for refusing office. He had evidently had enough of the council work. He declined to pay the fine, and was distrained on, and in 1839 he began an action against the council for illegal seizure of his goods. However, five months later it was reported to the council that he had not gone on with it. In the same year Mr. Ambrose Massey, having been elected councillor, claimed exemption on the ground of old age, and was excused; but why had he ever agreed to stand?

Local elections caused much excitement in those days, when they were a novelty, and the 1840 contest was very lively, according to the *County Press*, which said that "party feeling ran high, and hard words and harder blows were exchanged". But the decisive defeat of the Liberals disheartened them, and for four years they did not contest any seats. Then in 1846 they decided to fight again, and there was once more much excitement, which is described by Gibbs in his book on the corporation records. He says that the Bell was the Liberal house, and a meeting was held there at which about a hundred were regaled "at the expense of somebody". The *County Press* again made the accusation of bribery, and says that there was breakfast at the Bell and refreshments at

the King's Head for all doubtfuls. Transport was provided
to the poll, and Gibbs comments that it seems to have been a
very beery election. When the result was declared it was
seen that three Conservatives and one Liberal had been
elected, the Liberal being Mr. Shrubb, a ropemaker in George
Street, who had stood for the council unsuccessfully several
times. His persistence won its reward, for in 1849 and again
in 1852 he was returned unopposed. At the 1855 election
there was a real hard struggle, a genuine campaign, with both
sides issuing posters, which were very personal in tone. Some
of these state the amount of contribution the candidates had
made to a "soup fund", and argued whether or not a particular
candidate had recommended "turnip soup" for the poor in the
previous winter. The struggle was bitter, with no holds barred,
and poor Mr. Shrubb lost his seat, being bottom of the poll.
This appears to have been the end of his public career, for
the corporation minutes do not mention his name again.

After the first novelty of elections had worn off they became
tamer, and reached the lowest level on record in 1860, when,
according to the *St. Albans Times* (later the *Herts Advertiser*),
which had started in 1855 (four pages price 1½d.), only one
voting paper was handed in and the Mayor and his assessors,
having sat and waited an hour without any more voters
appearing, shut up shop and went home after declaring the
poll closed.

A problem which soon faced the new council was the
matter of public health. At the council meeting of January
12th, 1838, the town clerk reported that he had had a letter
from the Board of Guardians in the following terms:

To the Mayor, Aldermen and Burgesses of the Borough
of St. Albans. The Board of Guardians of the St. Albans
Union beg to call the serious attention of the Town Council
to the present unhealthy state of the Christopher Yard in
the hope that they will either by indicting the Owners of
the Property or by such means as they may think proper
endeavour to remove from the Town a nuisance that is
constantly endangering the health of the Inhabitants—the
crowded state of these Tenements occupied by ten families
chiefly paupers of which eight are now suffering under
Typhus Fever, renders the locality at all times, but more

G

particularly at this period of the year, a fruitful source of contagious disorder, liable to spread among a large portion of the poorer Inhabitants of the Town. From the reports of the Medical Attendant and the Relieving Officer of the District, and from a desire, if possible, of mitigating the evil, the Board of Guardians are induced to make this representation to the Town Council and trust they will not consider it unworthy of their attention.

Dated this 11th day of January 1838.

Geo. R. Martin,
Chairman.

The response of the council was laconic: "ORDERED that the Town Clerk do acknowledge the receipt of the communication and do make application to the proper Parties with a view to get the nuisance removed if practicable." The last two words sum up their attitude to the problem. The councillors had not yet become used to facing an electorate.

One of the clauses of the 1835 Act said that the municipality should have a police force. The first superintendent of police was appointed in 1836, a certain Alexander Wilson; he was assisted by several constables. A beadle was also appointed at an annual salary of £5, with a suit of clothes, waistcoat, breeches, coat, gaiters, shoes, stockings and a hat. The old police cells were still being used up to 1860, but they were in such a bad state that a prisoner died in one of them. It was proposed that some new cells be erected next to the Clock Tower, and that the lowest room of the tower be the police station, but an amendment was proposed that a piece of land near the Town Hall should be purchased for the sum of £120 and the police station built there. This amendment was carried only by the casting vote of the Mayor. Two months later the plans were accepted, and the small building just behind the Town Hall, now occupied by the City Information Office, was built.

Although the county had adopted the Police Act in 1840, four years after we had appointed our first superintendent, the county police force had no connection with the local force, which remained a separate body until 1948, when at last the two forces were amalgamated. There had been a scheme of amalgamation suggested in 1857, but the county demanded entire control and the proposal was defeated in the council. The next year the superintendent had resigned and was succeeded by Superintendent Pike, of Leicester, at a salary of thirty shillings per week, with clothes, to include duties of sanitary inspector, inspector of weights and measures, and of common lodging-houses.

There were certain disadvantages attached to this division of areas. The county force could not deal with any cases that arose within the borough boundaries, nor could the St. Albans police carry their activities outside their own area. Until 1948 the county police had a small station in an ordinary house in Fleetville, while the headquarters of the division were at Hemel Hempstead. Even today there are two benches of magistrates sitting at St. Albans, the county divisional bench sitting on Saturdays, and the city bench sitting on Tuesdays or Thursdays, and the cases with which they deal are divided as of old. The Mayor is *ex officio* a member of the city bench for his term of office, and until fairly recently he was, by custom, the chairman, even though he might not ever have attended a court before and be wholly without experience. That position was done away with, and now he is just one of the justices for the city. Similarly, the chairman of the Rural District Council and the chairman of the Harpenden Urban District Council sit on the divisional bench for their year of office. The chief difference between the two benches now remaining is that the city magistrates are not entitled to attend quarter sessions for the county, though they remit cases there exactly as do the county justices.

There are some old photographs of Hertfordshire policemen showing them in top hats, and many of them sprouting luxuriant beards and whiskers. Our police must have looked the same, and probably they were subject to much the same rules and discipline. The rules for the county police in the early eighteen-forties read strangely nowadays. They were not allowed to keep any livestock, not even the homely hen, nor could they leave their homes without permission when not on duty, though married officers could go to church with their wives wearing plain clothes; if they went alone, they had to wear uniform. Constables were graciously allowed to take their wives for a walk in plain clothes provided that they were not away from home above two hours, and someone was in the house to receive messages. Nothing is said about taking out one's best girl. Early police constables must have found it difficult to do a bit of courting. Even as late as 1890 they were not allowed to marry unless they had a certain nest-egg in the shape of furniture or cash. They wore their top hats and tailcoats until 1891. Though it is not certain that all this applied to the borough police, it is probable, following the rule of keeping up with the Joneses. It is unlikely that the borough would allow itself to be outshone by the county.

There are a number of police pay sheets in the city archives. One of them, dated September 30th, 1892, shows that there were a head constable, whose wages are not given, and thirteen policemen, of whom one was probably a sergeant, though this is not stated, but he is paid one pound eleven shillings and sixpence a week, while the highest wage next to that is one pound nine shillings and twopence paid to the two next senior men. The rest receive amounts ranging from one pound seven shillings and fivepence down to one pound two shillings and ninepence, which is paid to the two obviously newest recruits. This was for a seven-day week! Another sheet shows the position on October 12th, 1894. The sergeant's pay is now one pound thirteen shillings and tenpence. Perhaps he had been made an inspector. The next on the list, John Pike, was long remembered by some of the old folk as the much respected Sergeant Pike. He retired in 1910 on a pension of £68 per annum. In 1894 he earned one pound ten shillings and fourpence weekly. So did the other senior man. The next two men on the 1892 list were no longer in the force in 1894. One other had also gone, but there were four new recruits who had joined in the meanwhile. One of these was George Whitbread, who some years later was to become chief constable, and to live in the house attached to the new police station which was to be built in Victoria Street. The total wages bill for the week in 1892 was £17 0s. 8d., and for the week in 1894, £18 5s. 9d. There has been some little increase in police pay since then.

By 1909 wages had risen somewhat and a pension scheme

was in force. The head constable received a salary of
£192 6s. and the inspector £109. These figures appear in the
abstract of accounts for 1908–9, and the sergeant's and
constables' total pay was £1,703 14s. On top of this there
were clothing and holiday allowances, and the county council
was responsible for half the pay and clothing. But the city
council was not falling over itself in the matter of generosity
towards its police. In 1910 the head constable's salary had
risen to £200, a princely increase of £7 14s., the inspector
was getting £113; the wages of the sergeant and constables
had also risen by a total of £30, but the holiday pay had
come down from a total of £12 10s. to £12. This saving of
ten shillings, spread over all the force but two, seems a very
mean piece of cheeseparing.

There are many other references to the corporation's scales
of wages and salaries in the nineteenth century. A pay list
dated March 5th, 1887, shows that there were eight men
employed at the sewage farm. The top name, clearly that of
the foreman or superintendent, received one pound five
shillings for a sixty-hour week. Another man was paid for
fifty-six hours at 3½d. an hour, another did sixty hours at 3d.
an hour, another fifty-six and a half hours at 3d. an hour;
another was paid only 2½d. an hour. One man was paid
sixteen shillings for twenty hours' work, and one wonders
what his work was to be paid so much more highly than the
others. Another was paid eight shillings for ten hours' work,
obviously part-time.

There is another pay sheet of 1894 showing that at that
date there were thirty-five men employed by the surveyor,
and their wages ranged from one pound ten shillings paid to
one man only, down to fourteen shillings, all for a sixty-hour
week. There was also some piecework done, mainly at the
sewage farm, where the wages seem to be very low for some
of the workmen who did not do a full week's work. One
man or boy did nine and a half hours for two shillings and
ninepence, and two others got five shillings and tenpence for
twenty hours' work. One of these was H. Seabrook, and it is
allowable to wonder if he belonged to the family of the
eighteenth-century Mayor who tried to stick to the corporation
plate, whose name also was Seabrook.

By 1906 wages had not increased as much as might have been expected. There were then, in March, seventy-one employees listed on the surveyor's staff, the highest payment being one of two pounds, and the next one pound fifteen shillings. The hours were generally fifty-six and a half, and there was one woman, probably a cleaner, who was paid one shilling and sixpence for a time not stated. As a whole the wages of the council's workmen were still pitifully low. In the surveyor's annual report of 1913 the total wages bill of the manual staff, including highways department, cemetery staff, and that of Clarence Park and other open spaces, together with the attendant at the swimming baths and his wife, amounted to only £64 8s. 6d. weekly, and for that we bought the services of sixty-one people! The parks department employed one woman "for weeding, etc.". She earned, or rather she was paid, nine shillings weekly, and one would like to know just what was included in that "etc.". The abstracts of accounts give the salaries of the officials. In 1909 the librarian, *with his assistant*, received £116 6s. 1d. (the penny gives a delightful touch). It is not stated how this sum was divided between the two. The caretaker at the library was paid £60, which seems to be at a better rate than his superior officers. By the year 1910 the unfortunate pair were paid £124 0s. 10d., while the caretaker still received £60, so the differential had increased a fraction.

Our public library dates from 1881, when a committee, consisting of the whole council, and four gentlemen representing the school of science and art, was appointed, and a penny rate was assigned to it. The library and the school of science and art were established in the same building, and in this year (1962) the school of art is still there, though the county council is proposing to provide a new building in the near future. The librarian in the early twentieth century had a flat on the premises, and borrowers had to consult a catalogue to find the number of the book they wanted, and then study a huge fitment of small pigeon-holes into which were put box-like pieces of cardboard, each bearing the number of a book, and coloured one end red and the other blue. If the red end showed, the book was OUT; if the blue, it was IN. The borrower then asked for the number and the book was handed over the small counter to the left of the number board. As a child I always wondered how old people with imperfect sight managed to see the numbers on the higher rows. Probably few people now remember Mr. Plowman, with his venerable white beard, always so kind to me. I think of him with deep gratitude, for he introduced me to many books I might not otherwise have known. As a small girl I was rather a favourite of his. He had very little money to spend on books. In 1908–9 the fund for new books *and binding* was only £34 3s., and the next year, though probably the council thought they were being wildly extravagant, it was still only £67 2s. 9d. Books were, of course, considerably cheaper then, but even so the users of the library had very restricted choice of books, and many were almost dropping to pieces with hard wear.

As the city grew the old library became obviously inadequate, and Andrew Carnegie, the giver of so many libraries, came to our aid, and through his beneficence a new library was built, opposite the old one, in 1911. From the first it was an open access library, though many of the inhabitants wagged their heads and prophesied that the books would all disappear within a very short time from pilfering. The next step indicated is a move to a still newer and more adequate building in the Civic Centre or nearby.

We have not been over-generous in the payment of our officials. In the later years of the nineteenth century the surveyor was paid what seems to us a very small salary. In 1876, the year when the name of Sweetbriar Lane was changed to Victoria Street, the surveyor's salary was *increased* to £125. In the same year a medical officer was appointed. His salary is not stated, but he cannot have been very satisfied, for two years later the council had to appoint a successor, and his pay was £50 per annum. The 1876 rate, by the way, was two shillings and tenpence in the pound.

In the early twentieth century the salaries' account in the abstract of accounts is at first sight startling. The town clerk's salary is only £454 in 1909, and £456 1s. 2d. in 1910, but we must remember that at that date it was a part-time post, and Mr. Debenham, a local solicitor, had a private law practice also. The amount we paid him apparently included any clerical assistance he needed. But the surveyor, who held a full-time post, received only £200, and his clerk—apparently his whole office staff—had £100. The inspector of nuisances, the forerunner of the public health department, drew a salary of £137 10s. in 1909 and £140 in 1910. There was then no city treasurer, as the rates were collected by a local estate and insurance agent. It was not until after the Second World War that a city treasurer's department was set up.

One very interesting official is mentioned. That is the probation officer. The renowned Mr. Herbert Mundin was one of the earliest probation officers in the country. He was also the police court missionary, and one of the most interesting people of his time. No one can calculate the good he did and the influence he had on young offenders in the early days of the use of probation. He was the friend of all St. Albans. At £10 a year he was one of the best bargains the citizens ever made. His son, Herbert, became a stage and film star.

It was during the mid part of the nineteenth century that the hospital service grew from small beginnings. It began in a modest way in 1844, supported by private subscriptions. In 1861 a dispensary was set up in Holywell Hill, between Albert Street and Sopwell Lane, and on the site a small hospital was built in 1870. When, in course of time, that was outgrown, a site was obtained in Verulam Road, on the corner of Church Crescent, and the building was erected in 1887, which still forms the nucleus of the Church Crescent branch of the City Hospital, though of course, it has been considerably enlarged and modernised, and has taken to itself the old poor law infirmary in Normandy Road (formerly Union Lane, named after the workhouse which was sited at the lower end). In 1893 a fever hospital was erected on an adjoining site off Union Lane. This was the gift of Sir John Blundell Maple, the famous racehorse owner, owner of Maple's store in Tottenham Court Road and friend of the Prince of Wales, afterwards King Edward VII, who could often be seen driving through St. Albans on his way to visit Sir John at his house at Childwickbury. Sir John's family had suffered by the death of two little daughters from scarlet fever, and the hospital was built in their memory and was known as the Sisters' Hospital. It is no longer an isolation hospital, but has become part of the modernised Normandy Road branch of the City Hospital.

The hospital management committee had its headquarters in the early eighteenth-century house on the corner of Catherine Street and Normandy Road, which should, as remarked before, be called The Daltons, but unfortunately the hospital authorities saw fit to perpetuate the legend that it is the house which Dickens wrote about in "Bleak House". Of course, it is nothing of the sort. Dickens may have seen it, though there is no proof of that, but it is certain that he did not describe it in his book. None of the data he gives in any way corresponds to this house, not its appearance, nor its situation. In fact, if one studies the book, it would appear that if Dickens meant to describe an actual house it must have been on the London side of St. Albans, on the way to Barnet, and no such house exists or ever has existed which would agreed with the description. Dickens no doubt invented it, as he did other houses in other books.

To return to the middle of the century, there was another threat to the Clock Tower in 1861. A proposal was put forward to build shops round it. A local architect, a Mr. Hill, was the first prominent person to protest, but it was agreed on a motion seconded by the Mayor, William Simpson, and carried by six votes to three, that the shops should be erected, at the cost of a sevenpenny rate, and the Mayor was authorised to sign the contract with Mr. Miskin, a local builder, and founder of the present firm. But the Earl of Verulam and eighty-five of the clergy, gentry and inhabitants of the borough and neighbourhood signed a memorial to the council against the scheme. This shook the council, and the finishing stroke was dealt by the St. Albans Archaeological Society promising thirty pounds towards the restoration of the Tower (but only if the plans met with their approval). So the council's resolution was rescinded by five votes to three, and an appeal was made for funds to carry out the repair of the building. Two years later one of the citizens petitioned the council that the custom of ringing the curfew might be discontinued, but twenty-three citizens said that they wanted it to go on ringing, so the council declined to make any alteration. But the petition had set people thinking, and the next year another petition was presented, signed by twenty-six inhabitants, asking for the curfew to be stopped, and faced with this massive opposition the council ordered it to be silenced, and so passed a custom which had been carried on in St. Albans for over four hundred years.

By 1865 the public had subscribed £309, exclusive of the Archaeological Society's offering, towards the restoration of the Tower. Next year the council, in a wave of extravagance, decided to purchase a new illuminated clock for the Tower at a cost of £152. This was generous, for the next month they levied the rate of 9d. in the pound, and this yielded a sum of £828 2s. 3d. So the new clock cost nearly a twopenny rate. They increased the rate to 10d. the next year, but were able to reduce it to 8d. in 1868. In 1869 the rate was further reduced to 7d. and the rateable value of the borough was stated to be £22,772. The council was desirous of extending the boundaries, and proposed to promote a Bill for that purpose. A notification was received from the Earl of Verulam that he was opposed to the extension, and early the next year it appears that a public meeting had been held, at which some of the citizens had expressed opposition, one does not know on what grounds, but faced with opposition by both the nobility and the plebs, the council retreated from their position and the Bill was withdrawn. Extensions have, of course, taken place since, which have resulted in the boundaries as they exist today.

Now we must turn again to the story of the Abbey. As had been said by writers in the seventeenth and eighteenth centuries, it had become to a certain extent ruinous. Repairs had been carried on from time to time, and public subscriptions were collected to finance them, but the amount that was really needed transcended what the public were prepared to give. By 1870 the position was desperate. Sir Gilbert Scott had done some work on it earlier. But what was needed to save the fabric was a benevolent millionaire. It got the millionaire, but not exactly a benevolent one.

Sir Edmund Denison Beckett, later Lord Grimthorpe, a most remarkable character, who knew he was a good lawyer but thought he was an even better architect, and clockmaker, decided to join the committee which was pledged to restore the Abbey, and in his overbearing way soon he was virtually the dictator, inducing the committee to enlarge their ideas so much as to put them into serious financial straits. Here was his chance. He made a "take-over bid" for the Abbey. In other words, he used his wealth and his strong personality to overcome all opposition, and in 1880 he obtained a faculty which put the Abbey into his hands absolutely to make or mar at his pleasure. What he did with this power the Abbey now shows. The west front, certainly ruinous but possibly restorable, was ruthlessly pulled down, and it is both characteristic and ironic that the only monument in the Abbey to his achievement is his portrait bust as an archangel in the porch of the west front.

Lord Aldenham in 1888 tried to gate-crash on this orgy of "restoration" and applied for a faculty to restore the Lady Chapel, but failed in the attempt, Lord Grimthorpe's wealth turning the scale. The tragedy is that the restoration had to be carried out just when architectural feeling seems to have been at a very low level, and professional architects were perpetrating similar, perhaps even worse, travesties. And this must be said in defence of Lord Grimthorpe; had he not poured out his money as he did on his new toy, we should have no Abbey today, for within a short time it would assuredly have been completely beyond rescue. Alderman Miss Margaret Wix, the first woman Mayor of St. Albans, told me many years ago, that, when she was a girl, there were great holes in the roof of the nave, so that it was impossible to hold services there and the nave had been practically abandoned. Services were held in the Lady Chapel or more usually in the choir and under the tower. The people of St. Albans seem to have acquiesced in the alterations to their ancient building, and it is quite within the bounds of possibility that otherwise it would have been pulled down and either a Victorian Gothic church put up in its place, or maybe the site would have been sold and built over. All things were possible to the St. Albans of that day, alas! The citizens would on the whole have agreed with Lord Grimthorpe when he wrote:

"I confess I am sick of answering what I called the other day the modern cant about 'preserving the historical personality' of buildings. Happily the talkers and writers have a monopoly of it, for no practical man attends to it."

For us today the preservation of the historical personality of the city is a very practical matter, and many of us would give much for some of the buildings which Grimthorpe's "practical men" pulled down or outraged.

It was during the work on the Abbey that for the convenience of the builders the passage through the Abbey from north to south was closed. The citizens were affronted, and in 1874 there is an entry on the council minutes that a petition was presented, signed by forty-five inhabitants, against the stopping up of the highway through the Abbey Church, known as the Abbey Cloisters, and praying that the boarding recently put up might be removed, or in default the petitioners would consider themselves at liberty to take such steps as they considered necessary to enforce their rights. But the following week there was a counter-petition signed by sixty-three inhabitants in favour of stopping up the passage. So it was resolved that the passage should be stopped during the repairs, provided the work be completed within twelve months. But this was before Lord Grimthorpe with his sweeping ideas came upon the scene, and the work was destined to take many years longer. But many people felt very strongly about the closure, and on May 20th during the night, a number of citizens forcibly removed the barriers and re-opened the passage. The council met to consider further these doings, but broke up without coming to a decision. Later on there was a communication from the rector, backed up with the names of 158 inhabitants, and the council decided to let their previous resolution stand. The passage was, in fact, never re-opened, and the church authorities permitted the construction of the path round the east end of the building, which is used today.

It may be that the grandiose repairs going on in the church caused the government to remember that St. Albans had been intended by Henry VIII to be a bishopric, though this had not been carried out. In 1875 a Bill was passed to make the Abbey a cathedral, but perhaps because the repairs were not far enough advanced to make an enthronement possible, this did not come into force until 1877. Then the council petitioned Queen Victoria that, as the town had been made the seat of a bishopric, it might now be created a city, the bishop having recently been enthroned. On August 12th, 1877, a royal charter, our last, was granted, constituting St. Albans a city. Grammatically it should be the City of St. Alban, but the man who produced the actual charter wrote the City of St. Albans, and so it remains.

The archdeacon, who became Dean Lawrence, was so well beloved by the citizens that many years afterwards he was still affectionately known as "the Archdeacon", and as such I remember him. His portrait hangs in the Town Hall in token of the close connection between the Abbey and the city. The Dean is the Council's chaplain, and since, as the centre of the diocese, many public ceremonies are held in the Abbey, the council generally attend, as on mayoral Sunday, when the Mayor and Council go to the morning service with the civic flag flying from the tower. The Dean attends the opening of each council meeting, and, to quote the joke about prayers in the House of Commons, the Dean looks at the council and prays for the city. In my mayoral year I attended the Abbey officially nine times. The Abbey (few people call it the cathedral, except formally), occupies a special place in the city, being also a parish church, with ordinary parochial activities added to the diocesan ones. It no longer suffers from the neglect of past years, but always seems to have some maintenance work going on, and in the years after the Second World War much work was done on the restoration of the wall paintings.

CHAPTER SEVENTEEN

ST. ALBANS IN THE EARLY
TWENTIETH CENTURY

THE appearance of St. Albans differed considerably in
the early twentieth century from its look today. In
1900 there were no houses beyond the Crown Hotel in
Hatfield Road until one came to Oaklands, then a private
house inhabited by a Mr. Green, and later taken over by
Mr. Fish. The last Miss Fish died only a few years ago, but
Oaklands had been acquired some years earlier by the Hertfordshire County Council for development as an argricultural
college, and the original ugly Victorian house is part of the
administrative offices. Victoria Street was largely built up
during the nineteenth century, but as late as the early years
of this century there was no Trinity Church, and no buildings
between Upper Lattimore Road and Beaconsfield Road.
The former road was named after Cobden's friend, a farmer
of Wheathampstead, and Alma Road speaks for itself. Marlborough House, which occupied a very large site from the
back of the house now the Loretto College, to Victoria Street,
was the property of Samuel Ryder, head of the famous seed
firm, who pioneered in the production of small packets of seeds
for small gardens, who was a deacon of Trinity, the donor of
the Ryder Cup, a one-time Mayor, and whose building on
Holywell Hill went up during those years on the site of
demolished eighteenth-century houses, probably converted
from the remains of the mediaeval Bull Inn, which was on
this site.

Stanhope Road was tree-lined, and there was no Gaumont
Cinema. The trees were cut down when the buses to Hatfield
wanted to use that route in order to serve the Midland Station,
now the City Station. In St. Peter's Street, Hall Place was
demolished about 1907, and the present house built, with a
copy of the original gate, which had been sold, so it is said,
to America. Hall Place was a very interesting house. Part

of it was mediaeval in structure, though it had been altered during the centuries and after a fire. It had belonged to the family of Hall or Athall, the heiress of whom married in the fifteenth century, Edmond Westby, who was the host of Henry VI and Margaret of Anjou before the first battle of St. Albans. After the battle Henry returned to the house as a prisoner, and the owner in its last years liked to show the room where the king slept. In the reign of Queen Anne it was the country house of Dr. Compton, Bishop of London. After the demolition of the old house, the gardens and part of the neighbouring farmland were laid out in streets, and Townsend Avenue and Hall Place Gardens cover the site. Avenue Road was then a rough farm track, gated at the St. Peter's Street end, part of Townsend Farm.

Further down St. Peter's Street, several eighteenth-century houses were pulled down, and the Westminster Bank and Oakley's Stores went up, the latter having moved from the site in the High Street on the corner of Holywell Hill, occupied before their time by a draper's, Tresidder and Norris. This building was mentioned in the time of Edward IV. When Oakleys moved, Barclay's Bank expanded from the site already occupied by them on the west, and having demolished the old building, extended to cover the site, including that of a small shop round the corner, in which one had gone up steps to reach a chemist's shop.

On the west side of St. Peter's Street the Mansion passed out of the private occupation of the Misses Simpson, and shops were built into the lower floor. The upper floor lost its panelling and its very fine carved fireplaces, which were sold. There is a charming drawing of one of these fireplaces by Frederick Kitton in *St. Albans: Historical and Picturesque* by Ashdown and Kitton, which contains other most interesting illustrations of St. Albans as it existed when the book was published in 1893.

Behind that side of St. Peter's Street, towards the west, land once the property of the Kentish family, which had owned the Mansion and much land around the neighbourhood, was cut up into "Spencer Park", though no one calls it that nowadays, preferring to say Russell Avenue, Selby Avenue, etc. During the nineteenth century the old Gombards Field,

which extended north of the Kentish land, was cut up into
Church Crescent, Worley Road, Gombards, and, in the early
twentieth century, Etna Road was constructed and built up.
Worley Road was named after the Worley family, whose lake
in the meadows on the way across country to Park Street
was the only place where skaters could practise their sport
when the weather was suitable. Everybody went skating or
sliding "at Worley's" in the years before the First World War.
It was one of the Worley ladies who completed the building
of Christ Church, and she or another one gave the famous
fountain, which stood for years in front of the Clock Tower,
almost blocking the entrance to the Market Place. It fell a
victim to the increasing traffic through St. Albans when the
motor age began, and thereafter disappeared until in recent
years it was located in the garden of the restaurant constructed
out of the Water End Barn in St. Peter's Street.

The Watford Road was a pleasant winding, rather narrow
country way to our larger neighbour, almost unbuilt on, save
for the fine old house on the corner facing St. Stephen's Church,
with its garden extending a long way along Watford Road,
the little St. Stephen's school, two cottages almost opposite,
and some distance away the Three Hammers Inn, and still
farther off the Noke, then a private house, occupied for some
years by the manager of the ill-fated Birkbeck Bank, which
smashed in 1910.

At the foot of Holywell Hill, by the river, lived Mr. Hurlock, alderman, one-time mayor and a London business man,
whose house fronted up the hill, and through whose lovely
garden flowed the river, with a little bridge across from the
house. It made a wonderfully beautiful picture, viewed from
the road bridge, and was the scene of many open air charity
events and bazaars, for Mr. Hurlock was most generous in
lending it for charitable purposes, as was Mr. Ryder at Marlborough House. The trees backing Ver House were particularly fine, with some good poplars, which later on masked
the new housing estate developed off St. Stephen's Hill and
the gas works, but the view from the top of Holywell Hill,
one of the city's beauty viewpoints, was spoiled for ever when
the trees were cut down.

Up the hill, many of the old inns had vanished, leaving

only their names to yards. One which survived was the White Hart, but in the nineteenth and early twentieth centuries it was not so picturesque as today, as the added plaster had not then been removed, exposing the timber-framing. It was at this inn that St. Albans had its only recorded connection with the Jacobite rebellion of 1745. Lord Lovat, who was mixed up in the rebellion, was being taken to London for trial, and was taken ill (though the local physician called in to attend him considered that he was suffering only from panic at the thought of what awaited him in town), and he put up at the White Hart for a time. The doctor, named Webster, was acquainted with Hogarth, the great painter, and invited him to St. Albans and introduced him to the old rebel. Hogarth seized the opportunity to paint a portrait of him, which is preserved in the national collection. Tradition says that it was left to Dr. Webster, and after his death passed into the possession of someone ignorant of its value, and it was not discovered until eighty years later. It was bought for the National Portrait Gallery in 1866.

London Road was built up gradually in the nineteenth century, but the tollgate which stood across the road, just where Old London Road goes off to the left, approaching the city, was not removed until about 1890, according to a photograph by the veteran photographer Melbourne-Cooper which was taken about that time, and shows the tollgate still standing and a gate across Old London Road. The tollhouse, where now a garage stands, is shown falling into ruin.

The nineteenth and early twentieth centuries were great times for building new churches. First was Christ Church, which has an interesting history. When Diocesan House was the Verulam Arms Hotel there was a small pub next door, the Verulam Arms Tap. The hotel had become a private house by mid-century, and it was bought by Mr. Alexander Raphael, M.P. for St. Albans in 1848. He proposed to build a Roman Catholic church on the site of the Tap, with the house a centre for Sisters of Mercy. But he died before the building was finished, and the Catholics had not enough money to go on without him. So there it remained until 1857, when the property was bought by Mrs. Worley, of New Barnes, of the family before-mentioned, and she completed the erection of the church, the vicarage, and the school on the other side of Verulam Road, now the British Legion headquarters. But the church was not that originally intended; it was now Church of England. It was consecrated by the Bishop of Carlisle, and has the distinction of being the first church to be consecrated in the city since the year 1116, when the Abbey was reconsecrated after the Norman rebuilding. It is of unusual architecture, being of Italian design, and the only one resembling it in the country is at Kingston-on-Thames.

Then several Nonconformist churches were built. Dagnall Street Baptist Church made a second Baptist place of worship, the other being the Tabernacle in Victoria Street. The Wesleyan Methodist Church was in Dagnall Street also, but a new church was put up in Marlborough Road, and the site and building of the old church were sold to the printers, Gibbs and Bamforth, and became the printing works of the *Herts Advertiser*. Trinity Congregational Church came next, and the Catholics made another attempt with a building in London Road, but again lack of funds prevented them from keeping it up, and the site was sold, to become later on a garage. It was not until the early years of the twentieth century that they were able to put up a new church which could be supported sufficiently. That was the building in Beaconsfield Road, the Church of SS. Alban and Stephen. The growth of the city towards Hatfield into a district which acquired the curious name of Fleetville, made a church there desirable, and St. Paul's was built. The origin of the name Fleetville is this: Smith's printing works had to leave the Fleet Street area, and the new works were set up on the outskirts of St. Albans, being given the name of the Fleetville Works, which name extended to the district. The building, much enlarged, became the home of Ballito stockings for some years.

In 1868 a new county gaol was built at the bottom of Victoria Street, just across the railway bridge. All classes of prisoners were sent there, and executions took place. In fact, one of the last hangings was a woman. About 1924 it was decided to close the gaol and transfer the prisoners to other prisons. The city council acquired the property and pulled down the buildings except the great outside wall and the gatehouse. The space left inside the wall became the site of the city's highways department, as it is today. The gatehouse, which was the governor's quarters, is occupied by one of the highways officials. But many travellers arriving by train and watching the long line of very high wall as their train draws into the station, have been known to ask what on earth it is, and what treasures the city possesses to need such defences.

One of the features of St. Peter's Street is the line of lime trees, which adds so much to its beauty. They were planted in 1881 at the expense of a private citizen, Mr. H. Gotto, but the conditions were very different when they were planted, and modern road construction, which is impervious to moisture, starves them of water, and though they are artificially fed they are slowly dying. New young ones are not doing so vigorously as the old ones, and some time in the future St. Albans will find itself with rows of planes or maples, which will stand the drought and fumes better than limes. To picture the street without its trees would be unthinkable, so we can be glad that there are trees which, as proved by their London experience, will stand the hard conditions of modern times.

At this time in our history St. Albans was well—perhaps too well—served with public-houses. There seemed to be several in every street, making a total of at least ninety in the city, and as with the inns of earlier times they were even next door to each other in some cases. With so much temptation many more people appeared before the bench on charges of drunkenness than nowadays, when the charge is very rare. But the local bench must have been somewhat startled at one of the defendants one court day. To quote from *Judy* of November 7th, 1894:

"It is not a usual thing for a Mayor to be run in by his own police. That is what has happened at St. Albans. The Mayor was found by the vigilant guardian of the peace along with friends in a publichouse after closing-time. In due course he came as defendant before the Bench on which he was wont to sit as magistrate. His explanation was that he had 'called on a matter of business'."

A study of the photographs of the chief citizens displayed in the council chamber should suffice to identify the Mayor in question.

Mention of the photographs leads to the matter of the portrait of the Duke of St. Albans in the Mayor's Parlour. A good many people wonder just what this gentlemen had to do with the town from which he took his title. The answer is, nothing. There is a slight connection with Salisbury Hall, near London Colney, as his mother, Nell Gwyn, stayed there with the tenant, Sir Jeremy Snow, a friend of Charles II, who visited him at his home. There is a legend that her son was born in the house, and that she threatened to throw the baby out of the window into the moat unless he was given a title. Unfortunately for the lovers of legend, Charles, Nelly's son, was not created Duke of St. Albans until he was fourteen, and at that age his mother would have found it difficult to throw him anywhere. On the other hand, the title may have been suggested by King Charles' memories of sunny days at Salisbury Hall, from near which the Abbey tower can be clearly seen on the horizon.

The portrait, which is by Sir Peter Lely, was presented to the city council in 1888 by Vice-Admiral Vansettart.

The gold chain and badge worn by the Mayors in the photographs and by the current Mayor in the flesh was presented by an ex-Mayor, Mr. S. Monckton White, in 1885, for the use of his successors. It had then one row of small shields for the names of future Mayors, and some years ago a second row was added, as the previous row was full of names. New names are now engraved on the backs of the shields.

It was in 1899 that St. Albans acquired a museum. It is strange that a city such as ours should not have set up a museum years before, but the truth is that we did not set up one even in 1899; it was the county museum. One of those chiefly instrumental in its inauguration, and its first honorary curator, was Mr. A. E. Gibbs, the head of Gibbs and Bamforth, and when in 1961 the old museum building was enlarged and modernised, one of the galleries was named after him. The land was the property of Earl Spencer, whose family still have connections with the city, and he generously allowed the museum to be built on his property and to remain as long as it was still a museum, though if it should ever cease to perform that function the site is to revert to his family. There was danger of that happening some few years ago, when the county council announced its intention of ceasing to support it, but the city, which had contributed to its upkeep from the beginning, agreed to take it over and run it as the City Museum.

Sir John Blundell Maple, the donor of the Sisters' Hospital, proved again a benefactor in 1896, when he gave Clarence Park to the city. The Duke of Cambridge came to the city to open it. Apart from Bernard's Heath, handed to the city by Earl Spencer, it was the one open space the city had, and it became the centre of sports, especially perhaps cricket. St. Albans had for many years been noted for its cricket. It is said, I know not on what authority, that the first cricket club was set up in 1666, and that a match had entertained Charles II, when he came to the neighbourhood to escape the plague. I should like to think that the story is true. There is nothing inherently impossible about it. A code of rules was drawn up seventy-six years later. The St. Albans cricket was played on Bernard's Heath before Clarence Park was available, and there were giants in those days. Gorhambury contributed heavily to cricket personalities of the nineteenth century. The Hon. Robert Grimston was president of the M.C.C. in 1883, and he was the chief player in the home club. Earlier members of his family had occupied the same exalted post; Viscount Grimston was president in 1837, the first Earl of Verulam in 1840, and the second Earl in 1867. The St. Albans club was founded in 1876, and one of the founder-members was William Westell. He was also a noted member of the County Cricket Club. He was a member of the city council, being first elected in 1880. His son was another brilliant cricketer who, his son Claude tells us in an article in the *Hertfordshire Countryside Magazine*, had the unique experience of bowling W. G. Grace for a duck, appropriately enough at Aylesbury. Grace for ever after greeted him as "Aylesbury Westell".

Swimming has never received its due mede of encouragement. The first swimming bath was in Victoria Street, where the Salvation Army Citadel now stands. The baths moved to a site by the river in Cottonmill Lane, where a pitifully inadequate bath tries to cater for the many young people who want to practise this sport. In the early years of the twentieth century the council bought the house and grounds of one of the councillors in St. Peter's Street for the purpose of providing a swimming bath, but they received an exceptionally good offer for the land from London Transport, and an amenity which would have cost money like a swimming bath, however desirable, had to take second place to the chance of making money for the ratepayers. So we waited for many years for another chance. A scheme drawn up in 1961 for the council to construct a sports stadium near Verulamium included a good swimming-pool there, but nowadays the city has to ask the government for permission to spend its own money, and the proposal had to wait until that permission was given. Still, better late than never, and it was opened in 1971.

At the turn of the century the effects of the Boer War were felt, when a number of the young men sailed for South Africa in the local forces. Some never came back, but the city joined in the rejoicings at the news of the relief of Mafeking. There was a procession round the streets, and flags and bunting were displayed. But before the war was over the old queen died. That night the Oratorio Society was giving a performance of "Elijah" in the city, and at the interval the conductor came before the audience and told the news of the death of Queen Victoria. Then the orchestra played the "Dead March" from "Saul". I, as a very small child, was present at my very first oratorio. I had never heard the Dead March before, and I can remember how it impressed me.

It can be said that St. Albans was the cradle of the film industry. This was due to the pioneering genius of Arthur Melbourne-Cooper, born in London Road in 1872, the son of a professional photographer. When old enough, young Cooper joined the family business and formed a friendship with Birt Acres, and together they began experiments in "moving pictures". They produced a number of films, scenes of Barnet Fair, a woman cycling, and perhaps the first news film, the Prince of Wales opening the Manchester Ship Canal. Cooper soon began producing comic films, and to get money for more experiments showed them at fairs very successfully. As they became better known, he was showing them at places like the Crystal Palace, and at local assemblies and entertainments. As early as 1903 he filmed the Grand National at half-past three, developed the film in a special compartment of the train, and showed it at the Empire in Leicester Square in the evening. At home, he filmed a National Lifeboat demonstration (in which my father took part as a lifeboat captain, complete with my grandfather's naval spyglass), and showed the films at the old Drill Hall in the evening. He had the honour of giving a show before the King and Queen in 1903 at Chatsworth. The series of films called "Alpha Films" were taken locally, and local people were both stars and extras. He actually experimented in the making of "animated cartoons" long before the days of Walt Disney.

The next step was to open a cinema. The premises were found in the old "Poly" in London Road, where the Odeon now stands. This was a big hall where concerts, dances and other entertainments were held on week nights and "Poly Pops" on Saturday nights. The building was burnt down and Cooper took the opportunity to put into force his own ideas of the correct construction of a picture theatre. In the shell of the old Poly he constructed the St. Albans Picture Palace, where moving pictures were shown twice nightly at charges of 2d., 4d. and 6d. It was the first purpose-built cinema, and the proscenium was painted by the great comic, Fred Karno. It had all the newest ideas, tip-up seats, a sloping auditorium, and the dearest seats at the back. The patrons could not get over this at first, but thought they were being "done"; however, they soon found that they could see better from the back than the front, and every picture theatre built since has carried these features. The opening night was August 25th, 1908, and such great crowds came that hundreds were turned away, and "house full" notices were put up long before the performance was due to start, so Mr. Melbourne-Cooper's daughter told me. This great pioneer died in 1961 at the age of 88.

What was life like in those days before the First World War. The central point was, of course, the market. There had been a suggestion in 1889 to move it from the street and place it where the cattle market was until 1971. There is a map in the city archives showing these proposals, but they were not acted on, and the street market, the Saturday market, remains in its traditional place, though much extended. In the early years of the century, it went on for much longer hours than it does today, and on a dark Saturday night the scene was most picturesque, with naphtha flares glaring from every stall, and the figures of buyers and onlookers moving about in the gloomy patches outside the area of light, listening to the raucous shouts of the vendors. And it was very smelly with naphtha fumes.

In the market some of the traders were local, like the vegetable and fruit salesmen, and the occupiers of the meat and fish stalls. There were four or five fish stalls then, and they were set side by side by the pavement in the market place, opposite Timothy White's shop, as their predecessors were in mediaeval days. But the other traders were spread out, though even today there is a collection of vegetable stalls near the "Boot". Until later on in the twentieth century there was a stall placed in front of the Clock Tower, at one time a vegetable and fruit stall, at another a butcher's. Some of the stall-holders were great personalities. There was Mr. Turner (he was always "Mr."), whose son followed him in running the stall on the Square. If Mr. Turner could not sell an article he would say, "I'll smash it," and he did. The cleaners who had to clear up after the market, well into the small hours of Sunday morning, used to find sherds of broken china at the site of his stall. Then there was the man from London who sold clocks and watches, and very good they were. A clock bought in 1905 still tells the time efficiently in my hall, and another bought a few years later is now ticking in the dining-room. Then there were the costers who sold bedding plants. If you waited until the late evening, when they did not want to carry goods home, you could buy a box of stocks or anti-rrhinums, sixty seedlings, for a shilling, and a clump of delphinium, carrying half the countryside on its roots, for twopence. Of course, you had to carry the things home, but who cared? I once marched home carrying a garden fork proudly over my shoulder. It was still giving service thirty-odd years later.

The only theatre was in the County Club, off Waddington Road, and there the local drama societies and travelling companies used to entertain the public. Ben Greet came several times with his Shakespeare company, and performed "The Merchant of Venice" and other favourites. For many youngsters it was their first experience of a theatrical performance by professionals. For the more unsophisticated there were the occasional fairs held on the Gaol Meadow, and the Sunday School treats held at Gray's at Bricket Wood, where there was a permanent pleasure ground, and you could go on the roundabout or the swings or ride on a donkey. The City Band was an institution. As early as 1900 they entered for the national brass band contest at the Crystal Palace, and won the second prize of £10. The band used to practise in a little disused chapel room in Spencer Street, and it played in the market on Saturday nights. Of course it was in evidence on all ceremonial occasions, whether mayoral or trades union processions. It has now amalgamated with the British Legion band, so is keeping up the musical traditions of the past. The special processions used to attract much attention, especially the Whit Monday show. During the morning decorated cars and motor lorries, with tableaux mounted on them, used to perambulate all round the principal streets of the town, finishing up at Clarence Park, where races and competitions were held in the afternoon, and dancing on the grass in the evening. The band was always well in evidence that day. For those who wanted to go farther afield for entertainment, Hatfield House was open on bank holidays, and one hired a landau from Cable's the Jobmaster's in St. Peter's Street, and drove off in state. It was then unusual to find a great house open to the general public, and the Marquess of Salisbury was ahead of his time in doing so.

The cattle market was held then, on Wednesday—"Cow Day"; it was located on the square, and the air was filled with mooing, bleating and squealing from the different hurdle-enclosed spaces. The auctioneer had a movable rostrum, so that he could take biddings from near the animals being sold. There was one lot of animals which always attracted a great deal of attention because they looked so unusual. They were Highland cattle from Highfield Hall, and their long, spreading horns struck a quite exotic note among the shorthorns common to the neighbourhood. On that day the city was full of farmers in breeches, check coats and leggings, which they swished with their little whips as they talked. As there was no means of public transport until later in the century, they came on horseback or in gigs or traps or they walked. There are some fine trees growing along the roadside boundary of the Pré, and Lady Carbery tells us in her charming book, *Happy World*, that her mother, Mrs. Toulmin, had them planted to give some shade to the women trudging in to the market on a hot day from Redbourn. The horses and traps were put up for the day at one or other of the inns in their yards, and one saw the Red Lion and other inn yards full of them, more closely packed than cars in a modern car park.

At the present time the *Herts Advertiser* has almost a monopoly of local news, but there have been other local papers, none of which had a very long life. But the *Clock Tower*, which started in September 1895, and continued as *The Gazette* until October 1909, had a longer span of life. With its editorial staff was connected the well-known sporting journalist, Wagstaffe Simmonds, who lived in the city. Another paper which had a fairly long life was the *St. Albans Press*. This paper, which was run by Charles Sisley, came up against the monopoly of the *Herts Advertiser* and took a bold step. It became the *St. Albans Free Press*, and obtaining all its finance from advertisements, was distributed free round the town. It was a lively little paper, mainly made up of personal paragraphs, and it was a proud moment in the life of a citizen to find himself the subject of one of them. It lasted from September 1928 to February 1940, when a combination of war and the death of the founder brought it to an end.

Even in the eighteenth century St. Albans suffered from traffic difficulties. We remember the waggon of the councillor which damaged the market cross so badly that it had to be taken down, but when the motoring age started in the early years of this century, new and serious difficulties arose. One can hardly call the speeds of those early cars dizzy ones, but it was in 1908 that the first case of speeding in a motor car is mentioned in the corporation archives, and in 1912 motorists had become so daring that one of them had to be prosecuted for dangerous driving.

It is a wonderful change to find that by 1907 at last the city was beginning to take some pride in its history. It was a year in which there arose a craze for pageants. Every town of any antiquity had to have a pageant; it was a "must" that one had to keep up with the Canterbury-Joneses, and the rest. So we had a pageant, and a very fine one. It was held in the month of July, although it had been wished to hold it in June, the month in which St. Alban's Day occurs. However, Canterbury had already chosen the same week, so the organisers generously changed our date and put the pageant a month later. If ever generosity were rewarded it was then, for the week we had originally chosen proved to be a particularly bad one for weather; the other pageant was almost washed out, while we, in July, had a heavenly week, if anything too hot for the heavy clothes some of the performers had to wear. The pageant master was Herbert Jarman, and the very beautiful music was written for the occasion by W. H. Bell, Mus. Doc., the gifted son of a local tradesman, who had distinguished himself in the musical world. The Latin description of the city, sung by a large choir, was particularly lovely.

The pageant ground was where the other two later pageants have been held, an incomparable setting at Verulamium, and the enterprise was a huge success. So many visitors came, especially Americans wishing to take back a souvenir, that they started to take away bits of the Roman wall, and the Earl of Verulam, then the owner, was forced to put up an unclimbable fence along the length, a fence which was only removed when the Ministry of Works took over the guardianship of it at the time of the excavations of the nineteen thirties. There were many amusing and incongruous sights in the streets. Since there were no extensive dressing-rooms on the site for the very large cast, the performers dressed at home and walked or drove to the pageant ground, and one laughed to see a Roman soldier strolling along smoking a pipe, and a Briton in skins riding a bicycle. One saw an Elizabethan lady in brocade (probably the drawing-room curtains cut up), walking arm-in-arm with a cross-gartered Saxon in a yellow wig and long drooping moustache. It all added to the fun, and it brought trade to the shops and warmed the hearts of the shopkeepers. The ordinary citizen began to comprehend that there was something special about his city and something worth preserving. It was little enough, but it was the beginning of civic knowledge which leads to civic pride.

The year previous there had been the excitement of the general election, the landslide election, when the Liberals swept the country. There were big meetings at the old Drill Hall, in Hatfield Road, a huge place which held two thousand people, most of whom could not hear a thing, the acoustics were so bad. But one could see the famous speakers who came down to back the candidates. Sir Rufus Isaacs (Lord Reading) was only one of this galaxy of fine speakers whom we heard. In those days, voting was not all on the same day, and at the meetings towards the end of the campaign we used to hear the results of constituencies which had already voted, the meeting being held up to announce them. There was wild excitement at Liberal meetings when the defeat of some Cabinet Minister was announced. For the first and only time the normally Conservative St. Albans had returned a Liberal, Sir John Bamford Slack, at a by-election. Of course, he was defeated at the general election, but the Liberals felt that what had been done once could be done again, though it never was.

By 1909 we were getting the beginning of a system of public transport in the shape of a little bus which ran from market square to Fleetville several times a day. It was soon followed by another in the other direction, from St. Albans to Dunstable. Then the London General Omnibus Company took a hand, and we had a bus, open-topped of course, to Golders Green. To go up to Golders Green on the bus, stay on top, and return with the next journey, was an exciting excursion until the novelty wore off and we took buses for granted.

Education was making strides in the early part of this century. A school board had been set up in 1878, and from then on there were several board schools built, Alma Road, Hatfield Road, Old London Road, Camp School, Bernard's Heath and Garden Fields. These were all elementary schools, catering for all ages, for the school boards had no legal power to set up schools giving higher education. This was altered by the Education Act of 1902, which handed over the control of education to the county council. There was still no secondary school set up in St. Albans, although children might sit for scholarship examinations. The boys who won the very few awards went, most of them, to St. Albans School, at that time still known as the Grammar School, but the High School took only four girls a year as scholarship girls. The High School had been housed in the old hospital building in Holywell Hill, and was then one of the Girls' Public Day School Trust schools. Later it built new premises on part of the demolished Townsend Farm, next to the demolished Hall Place, and became entirely independent. Other than the four scholarship girls to go there, the rest went either to Luton or, more usually, to Watford Endowed School, later Watford Grammar School for Girls, and boys who could not get into St. Albans School, or for some reason did not wish to go there, also went to Watford to the Boys' School.

In 1913, though there were not any militant suffragettes in the city, there were many who sympathised with them, and there was a big audience at a meeting in the Town Hall when Lady Constance Lytton spoke of her experiences under the Cat and Mouse Act, and what it felt like to be forcibly fed. There was, however, quite a strong branch of the National Union of Women's Suffrage Societies, the non-militant society. In 1913 there was a great pilgrimage organised by this union, from all corners of the country, to end in Hyde Park at an enormous demonstration. One party came along Watling Street and arrived at St. Albans the evening before. Sympathising ladies, like my mother, put them up for the night. Next morning there was a meeting outside the Town Hall, and then the contingent set off for London via London Colney, all on foot. Some of us went with them, at least for a part of the journey, and then, the flesh being weak, finished the journey by train. That was on Saturday, July 26th. Only a year and some days later we were at war with Germany, and the suffrage movement ceased its campaign and turned its full energies to war work, to win its reward when the war was over and the 1918 Act was passed which gave the vote to women of an age of discretion, who had "a husband or some other furniture", as Ellen Wilkinson put it.

The First World War was declared on August 4th, 1914. The very next day a party of the Nineteenth Hussars arrived to be billeted for the night, a part of the 'contemptible little army" on the way to France. Not long after we heard that the city was to become the headquarters of a whole Territorial Army division, the Second London. Before the regiments arrived, officers came round the streets and mysterious chalk marks appeared on the lintels of the doors, figures which were found to indicate how many men could be billeted in that particular house. The 23rd London Territorials stayed with us for some time, then went to France and were replaced by the 20th London. When they had passed on to Gallipoli, other regiments from various parts of the country visited us for longer or shorter periods. Meanwhile, Napsbury Hospital had been cleared of mental patients, and became a huge military hospital with two thousand beds. Local churches and societies befriended the men when they were sufficiently recovered to be allowed to visit the city, and they seemed to enjoy their stay in the district. St. Albans shared the hardships experienced by the country as a whole, but fortunately the zeppelins did not come our way, though some of us saw the destruction of the one which fell at Cuffley, which was visible over many miles of sky. But in company with the whole country we all drew great breaths of relief when the Armistice was signed.

The East End of St. Albans Abbey in the 1920's

CHAPTER EIGHTEEN

ST. ALBANS AFTER THE FIRST WORLD WAR

ST. ALBANS, like the rest of the world, was a changed place when the war was over. The population had increased, and there was somehow a different atmosphere. The war had formed a break in our history. Politically the wind of change was felt, even though not yet very strongly. A branch of the Labour Party was born in the city. Its first important manifestation was in contesting a by-election in 1919. The candidate, who fought with an almost non-existent party, which made up in enthusiasm what it lacked in numbers, was John William Brown, a young intellectual who startled the city and the constituency by almost winning, being defeated by only 791 votes. Never, except in 1905, had the Conservatives come so near losing the seat. Nor, to be frank, did the Labour Party ever again come so near winning it until 1945. The Labour candidate, after fighting several times, took on some work which prevented him from standing again, and later became a highly respected county alderman.

By this time a social conscience was arising in the city. The poorer parts of the town were dire slums, a disgrace to any decent community, and in 1924 a meeting of interested citizens was held at Verulam House, at the invitation of the Bishop of St. Albans and Mrs. Furse, to discuss the local housing needs. A committee of enquiry was appointed to collect information, with Mrs. Furse as chairman, and the result, drawn up by Miss Cicely Craven, the secretary, proved to be a damning document. It showed that there were at least six hundred new houses needed to accommodate those without any houses at all, and many more were needed to deal with overcrowding, and still more were unfit for habitation by any decent standards. The enquirers were bitterly resented by those responsible for making money out of these slum conditions, and Miss Craven was referred to as "that damned amateur sanitary inspector". As the bishop wrote in his foreword to the report, "This report tells its own tale, and the tale is not one which any citizen of St. Albans can be proud of". Miss Craven was elected to the council, where she sat for three years. She was not the only woman member, for Miss Wix had already been elected, and in 1922 had been made the first woman Alderman. She followed that by being the first woman Mayor, in 1924. After her, there were to be no more woman Mayors until 1959.

In 1926 workers in the trades unions took part in the general strike. Some of the more timorous citizens wanted a corps of special constables to be enrolled to deal with riotous behaviour, but the chief constable is said to have told them, "If I want any riot squad, I can get all I want at ——" giving the address of the local strike committee. There was no disorder in St. Albans, though the members were loyal to their unions. By the nineteen-thirties the general depression was being felt in the country, but St. Albans largely escaped, and there was almost no unemployment. Just about this time the Earl of Verulam decided to sell a large part of his estate, mainly to the crown, but as some of the land for sale included a part of the site of Verulamium, the city council bought it and prepared to lay it out as a public park. The Archaeological Society of Great Britain decided to make as thorough an excavation as possible with the funds available, and a party led by Dr. Mortimer Wheeler and Mrs. Tessa Wheeler set to work on a series of excavations which were to last for several years, and to add immeasurably to our knowledge of Roman Britain in general and Roman Verulamium in particular. The series of annual reports which they issued are a most valuable contribution to knowledge, and the archaeological treasures which they uncovered, in the shape of mosaic floors, etc., made it inevitable that St. Albans must in the near future build a specialised museum to house them. This was opened in 1939, and has become world famous. When the excavations were over, the land which had been dug up was levelled and sports grounds laid out, while the meadow outside the wall was dug up and formed into a delightful lake. The work was done with the help of a loan from the Public Works Loan Board, and the council had to employ people from the dis-

The Norman Tower : St. Albans Abbey,
from the South-west

tressed areas.   Many of these came from Wales and the North of England, and they found St. Albans so pleasant that a number of them stayed here, found work, brought their families here and settled down, and today you may hear the most varied accents mingling in the market with the authentic Hertfordshire twang.

The nineteen-thirties were a period of change in the city. Traffic had increased so much that one of the Sunday evening entertainments was to stand on one of the corners of the Peahen crossing to watch the accidents. So when travellers brought back news of the new-fangled traffic lights that were being installed in the States, St. Albans was the first (or maybe the second) town in the country to have them, and certainly we were the first to have, a short time after, traffic lights operated by mechanism under rubber pads. For some time, until the novelty had worn off, it was one of the pastimes of local youth to step off the pavement and stand on the pads just to see the lights change. An amusing story is reported from the council at the time. The city engineer was explaining to the city fathers (and mothers) how things were going to work when the lights were installed, and one of the councillors, with a worried look, asked, "Mr. Mayor, is it a fact that in the future we shall all have to equip our cars with three coloured lights?". And the city engineer started to explain all over again.

In 1935 the council made an important purchase. Lord Grimthorpe had built himself a fine house at Batchwood, from which he could see the Abbey across his park. The story goes that he used to watch the work going on through a telescope. When he died the house passed into other owner- ship, and there were several successive tenants, but finally it fell vacant, and by that time few people were buying large houses; everybody wanted something smaller, in view of the shortage of domestic help. So the city council bought the house and grounds, and a public golf-course was constructed in the park, while the house became golf house and restaurant. The house is a fine one, its architecture rather surprising, con- sidering that it was built in the worst period of Victorian archi- tecture. It shows few signs of its date, and might well pass for a Regency building. The grounds are very beautiful, and the city has often been congratulated on the acquisition of the property.

Another feature of local life between the wars was the coming of branches of the great multiple stores. There had always been representatives of many of the grocery multiples, but now we acquired a Marks and Spencer, a Sainsbury's, and a Woolworth's, with some of the multiple shoe-stores, etc. Their erections necessitated the demolition of many of our fine old Georgian houses in St. Peter's Street, which, especially on the west side, lost its dignified aspect and assumed the non-descript look it now has. It was a great loss of beauty in our city, and unfortunately at that time there were no legal means whereby we could save some of these bits of our civic heritage. Even now the powers are not as adequate as one would like, in face of the danger to the physical character of the city.

The Second World War brought an acceleration of change with the arrival of some twelve thousand evacuees from London. It is pleasant to record that the citizens treated them well and in such a friendly fashion that many of them fell in love with the place, and became adopted sons and daughters who are still with us. Although there was some bomb damage and a few deaths from enemy action, the city did not suffer as much as many places equally near to the metropolis. Hatfield and Garston, for instance, were badly and frequently hit. The lake at Verulamium was drained to avoid reflecting the moonlight, though it was impossible to camouflage the tower of the Abbey.

Again a war made an almost complete break with the past. The St. Albans of 1945 differed in many ways from the St. Albans of 1939. New buildings sprang up. The housing situation became acute, and the city council had to embark on a big programme of council housing, which rose to four thousand houses in several new estates, St. Julian's, New Greens, Batchwood Drive, and London Road. The only obstacles to the continuation of this work are shortage of money, and, even more important, shortage of land. So much building has gone on since the war that the city is bursting at the seams, and built right out to its boundaries, where it is restrained by the green belt. The traders all seem anxious to pull down their old shops and rebuild them in the latest "contemporary" architecture, much of which does not fit well with the character of the city. In 1962 a Civic Society was formed to hold a watching brief on behalf of the citizens, and also to take an active part where possible to preserve what is still left to us and worth preserving.

The general election which followed the end of the war brought some shocks to St. Albans. With the revival of political activities it was found that the Labour Party had increased in strength to such an extent that for the first time a Labour Member of Parliament, Alderman Cyril Dumpleton, was returned for the constituency, though he later lost the seat to the Hon. John Grimston. But the Tories had had a severe shock. There was another shock at the city council elections, for as there had been no elections during the war, all but three councillors had to stand for election again, and in each of the three wards there were a large number of candidates. There was considerable cross-voting, with some curious combinations; for instance, on several papers the voters cast their choice for both a true blue Tory and a Communist! The result was that seven Labour members were returned, which, with the one Labour alderman, made up one-third of the council, which then numbered twenty-four.

Other things were moving with increased tempo beside the political parties and the traders and the builders. When the government began to set up new towns and extensions to old ones, five of these were in Hertfordshire, and the resulting increase of population caused the county education committee to plan a vast school-building programme, of which St. Albans had its share in the form of new schools, built in a new way, which was the admiration of the world, whose educationists flocked to the county to see them. St. Albans saw the rise of new secondary schools at St. Julian's and Marshalswick, improvements to the Sandfield School, and the foundation of a new County Grammar School for Boys in Brampton Road, and a corresponding Grammar School for Girls in Sandridge-bury Lane. Later still, a mixed grammar school was started in the old Alma Road School, to be moved later to a new building off London Road. Meanwhile, several fine new primary schools were erected, one of which, Aboyne Lodge, "the school in the orchard", was featured in the Festival of Britain Exhibition.

The only real mistake the authority made was in not making these schools bigger from the start, since it was not appreciated that many youngsters would tend to stay at school longer than the compulsory period, and, in fact, that has happened more fully in Hertfordshire than in any other county, so that many schools are over-full, and there are still old schools in the city which await modernisation. A later educational development in the city was the erection of the College of Further Education, which occupies a great part of the north side of Hatfield Road between Marlborough Road and Lemsford Road.

Throughout these years St. Albans School had been expanding. Much building went on, and the roll steadily increased, in keeping with its reputation. The history of the School in the past hundred years has been most remarkable. There had been an inquiry in 1866 which disclosed that there were then only thirty-three boys in the School altogether, and, according to Dr. F. M. L. Thompson (*St. Albans School in the Abbey*), the average age of the most advanced boys was only twelve and a half, and the tendency was for them to leave at thirteen or fourteen. The inspector reported that the boys entered the School very ignorant, and did not remain long enough to derive much benefit. Some fifteen years later the School was beginning to expand, but there were only about a hundred pupils at the beginning of the twentieth century. The rule of two headmasters changed all this. Major Montague Jones started the upward movement, and the scholars began to achieve success in university entrance. By 1931 the roll had increased to four hundred and twenty. It was in this year that Mr. W. T. Marsh was appointed, and his distinction as a headmaster brought the School to the position where, by 1962, the roll had increased to six hundred and sixty, and the record of its achievements in scholarship and athletics was one of which its pupils, present and former, could be justly proud.

In 1948 the three churches founded by Abbot Ulsinus in 948, St. Peter's, St. Stephen's and St. Michael's, celebrated their one-thousandth anniversary, and the citizens took part in another pageant. The script was written by Mr. Cyril Swinson, and he acted as pageant master of an impressive performance. The setting was again the space just inside the walls of Verulamium, with the existing Verulam block extended as a backcloth. It ran for a week, and there were some distinguished visitors, the chief being Queen Elizabeth, wife of George VI. Many people remember an incident of her visit. There had been very heavy rain during the afternoon —the performances were held in the evening—and just as she arrived the rain stopped, the sun came out, and a beautiful rainbow seemed to encircle the Abbey tower. It was the most spectacular effect that any producer could have dreamed of. The 1907 pageant had stopped at the visit of Queen Elizabeth I, but the millenary pageant went on to the constitution of St. Albans as a city. Other interesting guests were the Mayor and some of the council of the Danish city of Odense. This link was in memory of the adventures of the bones of St. Alban, as related earlier in this chronicle. Since then visits have been made by members of the corporations in both towns.

Another link with a country other than our own was inaugurated during the mayoralty of the fifth Earl of Verulam in 1956, when the city became officially linked with the city of Worms-on-Rhine, which has many features cognate to our own, being a cathedral city with Roman remains and certain industries. Visits have been made by corporations of both cities to each other's country.

James Brabazon, fifth Earl of Verulam, who first arranged this link, was one of the most remarkable personalities of this century. He possessed a brilliance so many-sided as to rival the personalities of the Renaissance. Linguist, classical scholar, scientist, an authority on housing, an engineer by profession, an archaeologist, a traveller to many lands on trade missions, a skilled cook, chairman of the National Baby Week Council (albeit he was a bachelor), known affectionately as Jim Forrester to the unemployed men of South Wales in the hungry thirties, there seemed to be no limit to his wide interests, yet he was as modest as he was brilliant, and when he died, at the early age of fifty, he was deeply mourned by the many who felt sincere respect and affection for him.

For many years one of the perennial sources of grumbling was the dissatisfaction with the train service on the main line railway. On September 28th, 1959, a service of diesel trains was inaugurated, and though the difficulty of unpunctuality seemed to be very difficult to overcome, the trains are now much more comfortable and cleaner than of yore.

After the accession of Queen Elizabeth II, St. Albans decided to celebrate the occasion with another pageant, a pageant of queens. Again Cyril Swinson exercised his great talents in writing the book of words and acting as pageant master. It was a tremendous success and attracted thousands of visitors to the city, and had a very great effect on the growing sense of pride in the history of their home which was becoming a feature of civic life. Since that time all sorts of voluntary societies want lectures on the history of old St. Albans, and anybody who knows about it is in constant demand. This is a most encouraging development and may, in the end, be the salvation of the character of our city.

During the next few years the city twice had the pleasure of being visited by Her Majesty the Queen. On the first occasion she came from Hemel Hempstead, where she had laid the foundation stone of a new church. She came from there to evensong at the Abbey. On the next occasion the royal Maundy money was distributed in the Abbey, the ceremony taking place for the first time outside London. The Bishop of St. Albans was the Royal Almoner. Large crowds gathered, and many thousands had the pleasure of seeing their sovereign that day.

CHAPTER NINETEEN

RECENT HISTORY

THE expansion of the old town of Hemel Hempstead into one of the new towns, with the industrial area by the ancient village of Leverstock Green, made the widening of the Bluehouse Hill imperative, and this was taken in hand, but part of it runs right through the heart of Verulamium, so the Ministry of Works arranged with the Archaeological Society of Great Britain to undertake a full excavation of the part of the Roman city which would be covered for ever by the new road. In the event, the excavations proved so valuable that they were carried on by public subscription when the road was completed, for it had in some cases cut through a house, and the government would not pay for a foot of excavation more than the actual area of the roadway. The excavations went on until 1961, and so rich were the finds, including what is possibly the finest mosaic floor in Western Europe, that the Verulamium Museum had to be enlarged to accommodate them. This museum celebrated its twenty-first birthday in July 1960. The occasion was marked by a lecture from Dr. Kathleen Kenyon (who had in the earlier operations excavated the theatre), with Sir Mortimer Wheeler in the chair.

The widening of this A.414 road was not the only road-making activity which affected St. Albans, for in November 1959 the M.1, the first of our motorways, was opened for traffic; branching from it was the St. Albans by-pass, long needed to ease the burden borne by the two trunk roads which passed through the city, the A.5, the Watling Street, which comes up Holywell Hill and goes on eventually to Holyhead, and the A.6, which passes through the city by London Road, Chequer Street and St. Peter's Street, and goes on to Luton and the North. These two roads caused great traffic difficulties, culminating at the Peahen crossing, which before the new road was opened was stated to carry the greatest weight of crossroad traffic in the world. If this was perhaps not strictly true, it *seemed* as if it were to us. Unfortunately, the M.1 has not taken as much traffic off our streets as we hoped.

About the same time as the opening of the motorway, there was another opening of great importance to the city. It was the inauguration of our first branch library. For many years we had used a mobile library to take the service to the outskirts of the city and ease the pressure on the central library, which serves a greater percentage of the citizens than almost any other municipality of its size, and the huge book-issue grows ever more huge year by year. The demands made on the mobile library showed that the greatest need was in Fleetville, and so a new library there was opened by Earl Spencer in October 1959. He performed the same ceremony in 1961, when the extension to the city museum was ready for use. It is pleasant to record his continued interest in the home town of his great ancestress, the redoubtable Sarah, Duchess of Marlborough.

The citizens can be roused on occasion, as was shown in 1958, when the Luton Water Company applied to the Ministry of Housing and Local Government for powers to establish a borehole at Bow Bridge, which St. Albans felt would endanger our water supplies. They wanted five million gallons of water daily from the valley of the Ver, and the water engineer experts whom the corporation consulted considered that it would seriously affect the amenities of the district. The Ver might dry up and there might not be enough water for the lake at Verulamium. A public meeting was held at the Town Hall, with an overflow downstairs, and a big crowd listening to the speeches on loudspeakers in the square. There has rarely been such indignant excitement, and the most vigorous opposition was offered. Altogether there were over a thousand listeners gathered to support the protest and the schemes for opposition.

Some very vigorous speeches were made. Lord Verulam voiced the general opinion when he called it, "A startling, scheming, stinking, stupid, strategem", and the crowd on the square outside cheered loudly. A committee set up included the Mayor, the Dean, the Chairman of the Rural District Council, Lord Verulam, Sir Mortimer Wheeler, and others representing the Chamber of Commerce and the Trades Council, with the support of the whole city. Never have the citizens been so united, and their opposition brought success. The amount of water the Luton Company was allowed to take was so small as to be almost useless to them, and the proviso was made that if it affected St. Albans in any way, they would have to compensate us by supplying water *out of that amount*. It was a real victory, and shows what St. Albans can do when all pull together.

In 1957 the city council decided to draw up plans for redevelopment of the area off St. Peter's Street, behind the Grange, as a Civic Centre, with a new town hall and block of council offices, and a new council chamber and committee rooms. The council offices were scattered in various parts of the city, and to collect them together would make for greater ease of administration. The county council applied for some of the land to build a new court-house to replace the old one, and a new police station, very much needed. A central paved square with shops was envisaged. Part of the site was owned by the company which owns the Odeon Cinemas, but with the drop in cinema audiences, which had become obvious, the land was offered to the council, which was glad to be able to round off its ownership of the whole site. The council engaged the distinguished architect, Frederick Gibberd, to plan the Civic Centre, and the first portion, a block of offices and showrooms, was opened in 1961. It was named Forrester House, after the fifth Earl of Verulam, who was so closely connected with the city, and who was Lord Forrester before he succeeded to the earldom.

The opening of the branch library did not bring the relief to the central library which had been hoped, and it was obvious that it was becoming very much too small for its purpose. When it had been given by Andrew Carnegie the population was under twenty thousand. By 1960 it was fifty thousand. In 1961 the library celebrated its golden jubilee with an exhibition and lectures, and a brains trust of well-known authors. The jubilee emphasised the necessity for a new central library, and the architect of the Civic Centre was instructed to adapt the plan so as to provide this, if desired, in the place of the now unwanted cinema.

In 1959 St. Albans started on a course which was to attract attention far outside its boundaries, a succession of three women mayors one after the other. The council has always made no discrimination on the score of sex, and a number of the chief officers have been women, including the first woman town clerk, the chief librarian and the director of museums, but there had been no woman Mayor since Alderman Margaret Wix in 1924, and this new development seemed a triumph of fairmindedness on the part of the city fathers. In fact, the city itself was quite unmoved, and has always taken for granted responsibility in public affairs on the part of women. I had the honour of being the second of the three Mayors, and the third woman Freeman.

In January 1961 there occurred the quatercentenary of the birth of Francis Bacon, and the city celebrated it suitably. There was a service at St. Michael's Church, where his memorial is, and it was attended by people famous in law, literature and science, including the Lord Chancellor himself (Lord Kilmuir), resplendent in robes, full-bottomed wig and knee-breeches, carrying the famous embroidered bag, with his train carried by his page. Lord Salisbury, robed in scarlet, read the lesson, and Professor Hugh Trevor-Roper gave a brilliant address. The council attended in state. The service was followed by an exhibition which lasted for a week, and drew a large number of visitors.

One other great event happened in 1961. St. Albans has never been lavish in creating freemen, perhaps remembering when the freedom was bought and sold in the bad old days of the eighteenth century, but now the corporation decided to invite Queen Elizabeth the Queen Mother to become an honorary freeman, as she was born in the county and was not a freeman of any other municipality of the county. She was graciously pleased to accept, and a most happy occasion was enjoyed by thousands on April 13th, when she came, first to the Abbey, then to Batchwood for luncheon, and finally to the Town Hall, where she reviewed a guard of honour from the Hertfordshire Regiment, of which she is honorary colonel, and then entered the Town Hall to sign the roll and receive the scroll of the freedom, inscribed by a local artist, in a silver and crystal casket, designed and made by a local silversmith.

The very happy Mayor on the momentous occasion was myself.

Every town has its few eccentrics who cannot be bound in the ordinary conventional chains, and they should be mentioned somewhere in this book. There was the old lady who lived in Hall Place before the old house was demolished, and who went about the city looking like a tramp, in clothes which no self-respecting rag-and-bone man would consider making an offer for, yet who in the evening changed into full evening dress, put on her jewels and dined, waited on by her butler and parlourmaid. There was the corn chandler of St. Peter's Street who attended St. Peter's Church, and whenever he had to stand for hymn, psalm or creed, turned his back on the altar and spoke to the back of the church. These flourished in the early part of the twentieth century. Then there was our poet, Herbert Palmer, who was for a time a master at the St. Albans School, but who suffered in the way that possibly the other poet, James Shirley, suffered so long before him. He gave up teaching, and lived on the proceeds of his poetry, which was highly thought of in literary circles. He was granted a civil list pension and wrote a most useful book on the teaching of English. He was a personality that could not be ignored, as the tall, painfully thin figure went at a rapid shamble through the streets with his string bag, rarely recognising anybody, but obviously lost in his own thoughts. How he escaped death when he crossed the road without looking for traffic was a puzzle to all his friends. He would speak in the debating society in an impassioned tone, a dedicated man. He could not have survived to over seventy without the loving care of his sweet wife, who deserved a saint's halo. His best-known poems were published in a collected edition in 1933.

In the years which have elapsed since 1962, momentous things have happened to this ancient city. The growing weight of traffic which was strangling the streets which were the heritage left by Abbot Ulsinus and his fellow-abbots, made some controls necessary, and the traders were meeting growing competition from the newer centres of commerce in the neighbouring towns. So the Council decided to go ahead with the development of the Civic Centre, with a good concert hall, a new central library, and comprehensive block of municipal offices with a new Council Chamber, away from the distracting noise of the market place and Chequer Street. At the same time the county council found it urgently necessary to build the new large police station and a new law court with four courts in place of the one noisy court in which I had served so many years.

So the county asked the city to sell them some of the land cleared for the Civic Centre, and, with complete indifference to the feelings of many of the citizens, suggested that they would be willing to take the old Town Hall off the Schedule of Listed Buildings so that we could build a supermarket in its place. This roused a storm of protest in the breasts of those like me, who cared for the quite good George Smith building of 1829, which provided a perfect close to the view down St. Peter's Street, and without which the heart of the city would become an artistic wreck. I spoke my mind very forcibly to the B.B.C. interviewer who came to talk to me about the horrible suggestion. Those who felt like I did told the county that unless they paid more attention to our standpoint, they would not get any of our land for their grandiose schemes. We said, "That land is ours—freehold, and not a brick do you put on it until we have settled the matter of the old Town Hall." The Town Clerk took opinion, and it was established that the city had inalienable rights to much of the old building, and that the county had no power to dispose of more than a part of it. So in the end, a deal was done with the county which acquired the land they wanted, and the city, by paying a comparatively small sum, retained the old hall. The county built a monstrosity of a police station, which has an entrance up so many steps that no disabled person can climb up there. The other buildings are more innocuous, but too few courts were built, and those that were are very cramped, and the acoustics are such that the merest whisper from one Justice to another can be clearly heard by the back row of the public seats.

The new City Hall has been a great success, and, seating about a thousand, has given the citizens a chance of hearing some of the finest musicians of the day.

Traffic is always a problem here, and many schemes have

been put forward to deal with it without destroying the character of our city, none of them wholly satisfactory. Light-controlled pedestrian crossings make it safer to cross St. Peter's Street, but destroy the visual spaciousness of the Market Square with railings. But the plans committee backed up by the council have been more successful than other Hertford-shire towns in preserving the spirit of the city, and keeping so many of the historic buildings.

A change has taken place in the government of the area. Some few years ago a committee headed by Lord Maud, issued a report on the "reform" of Local Government, and obsessed with the idea that "Bigger is Better" proposed sweeping changes all over the country. Our fate was to be to lose our city status and be joined up with, not only the rural district, which was bearable and sensible, but also with Harpenden, and of all places, Luton. It ignored the Scriptural exhortation about not being unequally yoked together. Hertfordshire, as a county was to vanish and be cut up into three pieces—never mind its history of more than a thousand years. The baby was to be not only thrown out with the bath-water, but drowned first.

However, wiser opinions prevailed. The county remained inviolate, and the city was left to settle down, after the inevitable teething troubles, with its neighbours the rural district and Harpenden, as the City and District of St. Albans, on April 1st. 1974. Let us hope that the inaugural date is not an omen of its future.

And now the tale of St. Albans has been carried up to the year 1975. It has had a past chequered with honour and disgrace, with excitement and quietude, but the honour has predominated. We have shown honour to great men and women, and hospitality to pilgrims and help to refugees. As has already been told, the town showed its charity when the pitiable crowd of prisoners from Colchester came here in the Civil War, and to show that their descendants are no less merciful the city raised in the world refugee year of 1959–60 the sum of £8,000 for help to the miserable victims in the Second World War, still enduring life in refugee camps. In fact, while I was Mayor, I was impressed by the tremendous number of societies of every kind existing in the city, many of them devoted to helping the unfortunate, societies to help the blind, the deaf, the physically handicapped, the mentally handicapped, the old folk, and the voluntary work done for youth clubs. There are, of course, gatherings for social enjoyment, but so many of the organisations have also an aspect of service to the community. The Rotary Club, the Round Table, the Ladies' Circle, the Soroptimists, the Business and Professional Women's Club, the very numerous branches of the Federation of Women's Clubs, the equally numerous Young Wives' Clubs of the churches (and Mothers' Unions) all have serious aims, and are not merely for enjoyment. Other societies have educational aims, such as the Workers' Educational Association and the Debating Society, while the evening classes of the College of Further Education number their students in thousands.

We still have many tasks before us. We have to complete the Civic Centre, and when this is done we shall have development of which any city can be proud. We have to deal with the ever-increasing traffic problem, and must find places where multi-storey car parking can be provided. The centre of the city should be redeveloped in accordance with the character of the place, while preserving all of the old that can be preserved. The corporation has shown the way by restoring French Row and Mayle's Corner and Pemberton Almshouses, while returning some old houses in Fishpool Street to useful life and continuing occupation. The plans committee of the city council is one of the principal agents in such good work, for by refusing permission to develop in a way that is unsuitable, such buildings which would spoil our city are in many cases avoided, though the powers in this direction are not as great as could be wished. But no one would desire that the city should become a beautiful fossil; it is a city which, though casting proud glances backwards, turns its eyes also forwards to the future, that it may do as the citizens in the past have done—leave behind a city of which posterity also may be proud.

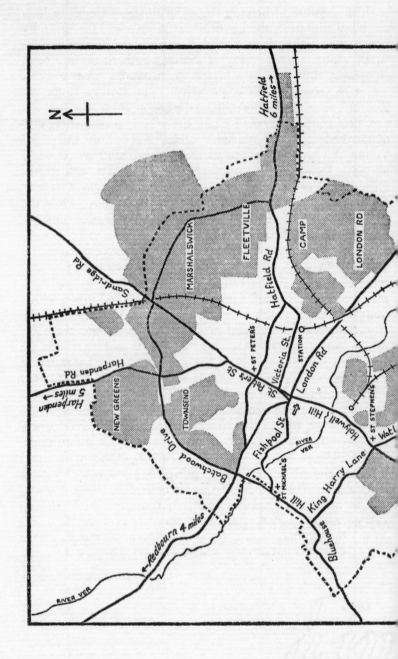

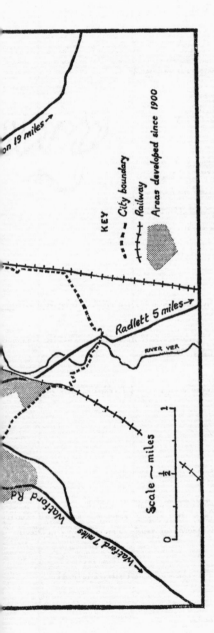

A SKETCH-MAP SHOWING THE GROWTH OF ST. ALBANS IN THE TWENTIETH CENTURY

In 1901, when the area within the city boundary was 997 acres, the population was just over 16,000, living mainly in the old central part of the town and St. Michael's. With subsequent extensions of the boundary the area of the city is now 5,129 acres, and the population (from the latest figures available) now exceeds 50,000. The sketch-map shows the present boundaries of the city, and the areas where there have been large-scale development, much of it by the City Council, between two wars and since the end of the Second World War.

BIBLIOGRAPHY: A SELECTION

A.

UNPRINTED SOURCES

In St. Albans City Archives:

>*Minutes of Council Meetings.*
>*Mayors' Accounts.*
>*Charters.*
>*Deeds relating to the Clock Tower.*
>*Deeds relating to the Stone House.*
>*Miscellaneous papers and maps.*

In the County Record Office, Hertford:

>*Records of Quarter Sessions,*
>*County and Liberty.* (*Originals, but calendared.*)
>*Archdeacons' Registers of Wills.*
>*Gape Papers.*
>*Gorhambury Papers.*

Report on St. Albans: Society for the Protection of Ancient Buildings, 1945.

Marian Survey of St. Albans, in Augmentation Office. Public Record Office Miscellaneous Books, Vol. 391.

Parish Registers. Various.

James West, M.P. An unpublished Essay, by Lt.-Col. John H. Busby, 1960.

B.

PRINTED SOURCES

Reports on the Excavations at Verulamium, 1931 to 1961.
Records of the Abbey Chroniclers, in Rolls Series: *Matthew Paris, Rishanger, Walsingham, Wheathampstead, Trokelowe, Blaneford.*
Close Rolls.
Patent Rolls.
Calendar of Letters and Papers, Foreign and Domestic, 1509–41.
Bede's *Ecclesiastical History.*
Herts Notes and Queries. 1895–8.
Parliamentary Elections: Poll Books.

Parliamentary Commission: *Enquiry into Bribery at St. Albans*, 1852.
Transactions of the St. Albans Architectural and Archaeological Society,
    Various dates from 1892.
Herts Advertiser from 1855.
Dugdale: *Monasticon*.
Gibbs: *Corporation Records*, 1890.
Gibbs: *Records of St. Albans School*, 1888.
Shaw: *History of Verulam and St. Albans*, 1815.

C.

OTHER WORKS

Nicholson: *History of the Abbey of St. Albans*, 1879.
Rushbrooke Williams : *History of the Abbey of St. Albans*, 1917.
Victoria County History of Hertfordshire, Vol. 2, 1902.
Levett: *Studies in Manorial History*, 1938.
Snape: *Monastic Finance*, 1926.
Jenkins: *The Monastic Chronicler and the Early School of St. Albans*,
    1922.
Savine: *English Monasteries on the Eve of the Dissolution*, 1906.
Gasquet: *Henry VIII and the English Monasteries*, 1906.
Froude: *Short Studies*, Third Series, 1887.
Hertfordshire Countryside Magazine. Articles of various dates.
Abbey Papers, 1., Vaughan: *Matthew Paris*, 1958.
Abbey Papers, 2. F. M. L. Thompson: *St. Albans School in the Abbey*,
    1960.
Chauncy : *Historical Antiquities of Hertfordshire*, 1700.
Illustrations of the Life of St. Alban, ed. Lowe, Jacob and James, 1924.
Galbraith: *The St. Albans Chronicle*, 1937.
Urwick: *Day School Education in St. Albans*, 1888.

There is a collection of local history books, prints, etc., in the
St. Albans Room at the City Central Library.

ABBOTS OF ST. ALBANS ABBEY

1. Willegod, *c.* 793
2. Eadric   *(Dates unknown)*
3. Wulsig   ,,
4. Wulnoth   ,,
5. Eadfrid   ,,
6. Ulsinus or Wulsin   ,,
7. Alfric   ,,
8. Aldred   ,,
9. Eadmer   ,,
10. Alfric II, *c.* 970–990
11. Leofric, 990–*c.* 1042
12. Leofstan, 1042–1064
13. Frederic, 1064–1077
14. Paul de Caen, 1077–1097
15. Richard d'Essai or Albini, 1097–1119
16. Geoffrey de Gorham, 1119–1146
17. Ralph de Gobion, 1146–1151
18. Robert de Gorham, 1151–1167
19. Simon, 1167–1183
20. Warin, 1183–1195
21. John de Cella, 1195–1214
22. William de Trumpington, 1214–1235
23. John de Hertford, 1235–1263
24. Roger de Norton, 1263–1290
25. John de Berkhamsted, 1290–1301
26. John de Maryns, 1302–1309
27. Hugh de Eversden, 1309–1327
28. Richard de Wallingford, 1327–1336
29. Michael de Mentmore, 1336–1349
30. Thomas de la Mare, 1349–1396
31. John Moote, 1396–1401
32. William Heyworth, 1401–1420
33. John of Wheathampstead, 1420–1440
34. John Stoke, 1441–1452
    John of Wheathampstead re-elected, 1452–1465
35. William Albon, 1465–1476
36. William of Wallingford, 1476–1492
37. Thomas Ramryge, 1492–1521
38. Thomas Wolsey, 1521–1530
39. Robert Catton, 1531–1538
40. Richard Boreman of Stevenage, 1538–1539

INDEX

Aaron of Lincoln, 34
Abbey Church, Condition in
    17th c., 110–112
    Condition in 19th c., 139
    Restoration, 162–164
    Closure of passage, 164
    Cathedral, 164–65
Abbey, 11, 13, 21, 22, 23, 27, 29,
    36, 40, 41, 42, 47, 64, 67
    Life in, 29–33
    Dissolution, 68–69
Adam the Cellarer, 27–28
Agricola, 6–7
Alban, St., 10–11
Aleward, William, 112
Alfric, Abbot, 16
Anketil, 25, 26
Angell the carpenter, 84
Anselm, Archbishop of Canter-
    bury, 23
Attewelle, Alice, 74–75

Bacon, Anthony, 96
    Lady Anne, 97
    Sir Francis, Baron Verulam,
    96–99, 195
    Nathaniel, 114
    Sir Nicholas, 84, 86
Ball, John, 54
Baskerville, Thomas, 111–112
Batchwood, 186
Battles of St. Albans, 60–62
Bede, The Venerable, 11–12
Belgae, 1, 2, 4
Belvoir, Cell at, 22
Benefit of Clergy, 81
Berkhamsted, Roger of, Abbot,
    47

Binham, Cell at, 22, 38
Bishopric, 164–165
Black Death, 50–51
Black Prince, 51, 52
Bleak House, 161
Book of St. Albans, 63
Boreman, Nicholas, printer, 63
Boreman, Abbot Richard, 67,
    68, 69
Boudicca, 5
Bowley, Mary, 134–135
Breakspear, Nicholas, 26, 27
Breauté, Faulkes de, 40
Bribery at St. Albans, 116–123,
    132
Brown, John William, 183
Bull Inn, 111–112

Caen, Abbot Paul de, 21–22
Canute, 17
Caratacus, 4
Cassivellaunus, 2
Catton, Abbot Robert, 66, 67
Cella, Abbot John de, 35, 36, 38,
    39
Charities, Clark's, 124
    Marlborough, 126–127
    Pemberton, 82, 109
    Raynshaw, 79
Charles, I, 104
Charles II, 107
Charnel House, Brotherhood of,
    68–69
Charters, Henry IV, 58
    Edward VI, 82; Mary I,
    83; Elizabeth I, 83;
    Charles II, 106, 116;